The Captive in Patagonia by Benjamin Franklin Bourne

or, LIFE AMONG THE GIANTS

A PERSONAL NARRATIVE

HUNTING THE GUANACHO

On our precious globe, oceans spill their majestic waters across 70% of the Earth's surface. Over the continents, land untainted by the presence of man is becoming ever more elusive and scarce.

One area that almost retains its pristine, unspoiled look is Patagonia in South America.

This sparsely populated region is located at the southern end of South America and displays itself across the vast lands of Argentina and Chile. As a whole it comprises of the southern section of the Andes mountains as well as the deserts, pampas and grasslands east of this. Patagonia has two coasts: to the west it faces the Pacific Ocean and to the east the Atlantic Ocean.

The Colorado and Barrancas rivers, which run from the Andes to the Atlantic, are commonly considered the northern limit of Argentine Patagonia. For Chilean Patagonia it is at Reloncaví Estuary. The archipelago of Tierra del Fuego marks its abrupt southern frontier and the famed end of the world.

The name Patagonia comes from the word patagón, which was used by the Spanish explorer Magellan in 1520 to describe the native people that his expedition thought to be giants. He called them Patagons and, we think now, they were from the Tehuelche people, who tended to be taller than Europeans of the time.

Patagonia encompasses some one million square kilometers and is home to a rich and diverse landscape of plants, fauna and wildlife. It is a spectacular wilderness full of life and full of history.

Early explorers and travellers faced a sometimes difficult and uncomfortable journey to reach there. The words and pictures they brought back bear testament to a remarkable land and remarkable people.

These are their stories.

Index of Contents

THE CAPTIVE IN PATAGONIA

PREFACE

Book-making is so much of a trade, that it may be thought quite unnecessary to be at the trouble to assign reasons for embarking in it; but, as it is not my own vocation, it will be allowed me to say, that the deep interest which many, not only of my personal friends, but others whom I never saw, have taken in my fortunes, and the desires expressed, both verbally and by letter, to know more of my adventures than was communicated through the newspapers, overcame the reluctance I felt to undertake such a task. The interest of personal adventure, however, great as it might be in immediate view of the events while they were fresh, would not alone have been presumed upon as a sufficient attraction for this volume. But the strangeness of the country observed, and the deficiency of exact information concerning its people, it was thought, would make welcome any contribution, however slight, to the knowledge of this section of our world and race. After the contradictory statements of voyagers as to the "giants" of South America, there may be some curiosity to hear the testimony of one who has "seen the elephant" under circumstances that enabled him to measure its proboscis.

My story is a plain one,—a simple record of facts, but not, I would hope, tedious. It offers no feats of literary agility for the critic's inspection, but a recital of human experiences and observations, sufficiently aside from the beaten track of life to have attracted a degree of attention which flatters me with the belief that they will repay a nearer and more minute survey.

CHAPTER I

For California—Pernambuco—Straits of Magellan—Trading with Patagonians—Their treachery—Four men made prisoners by them—Three escape; the author detained, with promises of release on paying ransom—Indian village—The chief and his household—Eating, sleeping, and adventure in a Patagonian wigwam—Find myself booked for an indefinite residence in Patagonia, and some natural reflections thereupon.

Among the early subjects of the "gold fever" that became epidemic in the autumn and winter of 1848-9, a company of twenty-five men left the port of New Bedford in the schooner John Allyne, A. Brownell, master, and B. F. Bourne, mate, for California. The vessel had been selected for her good sailing qualities, light draught of water, and general fitness for river navigation. In the haste and excitement of the time, California-bound craft carried out some rather motley companies; but we considered ourselves fortunate in the character of the men associated in this enterprise, and were organized on such principles of equality as seemed to promise entire harmony and good fellowship. Of course we had high and golden hopes, and our great object was to reach the new Ophir in the easiest and most expeditious manner. On account of the delays and dangers incident to the doubling of Cape Horn, it was determined to attempt the passage of the Straits of Magellan.

We left port on the 13th of February, and for many days our time passed pleasantly, but rather monotonously, with nothing greatly to exhilarate or to depress our spirits. It was discovered, at length, that our vessel needed some running rigging. The more impatient were for going on, and making such headway as we could without it; but a majority of the company decided to run for the nearest convenient port, and replenish. We accordingly ran for Pernambuco, and anchored in the outer harbor on the 25th of March. The beauty and security of this harbor are remarkable. It is defended from the sea by a nearly perpendicular reef, extending three-fourths of the way across its entrance, with an opening of ample width for the passage of vessels to a safe anchorage. Being but eight degrees south of the equator, the town lies continually under the burning rays of a tropical sun. Its appearance is like that of most Spanish and Portuguese cities, abounding in high and massive buildings, with more of the castle than of the counting-house or dwelling in their outward expression, built upon narrow, irregular streets, that are constantly alive with men and beasts of divers colors and forms. Men from the country, driving their mustangs, mules and asses, laden with produce; wealthy and noble citizens borne by servants in palanquins; women bearing water in buckets, tubs and urns, which they balance on their heads without the aid of their hands, and walk off under as erect as so many midshipmen;—all the sights and sounds have a pleasant strangeness, that made our visits on shore highly agreeable. The churches, which are quite numerous, have nothing admirable or attractive outside, but the richness of their interior decoration testifies to the prevailing orthodoxy and fervor of devotion to the Church of Rome. The church is, indeed, the grand receptacle of the wealth of the country. Every bueno católico of them, rich, or poor, will sooner stint himself and his family in their daily comforts, or even necessaries of life, than omit his due contribution to mother church.

Our stay at Pernambuco was short, which must excuse a more particular description of its notabilities. Having obtained the articles we needed, we stood out to sea. Nothing occurred on our passage to the straits worthy of particular record. We spoke one or two vessels, and spent some time "gaming" with them,—the nautical phrase for visiting. On the 30th of April we made Cape Virgin, and stood in for the Straits of Magellan. In company with us, and bound for the same golden country, by the same course as ourselves, were bark Hebe, of Baltimore, and schooner J. B. Gager, of New York. We were becalmed off the mouth of the straits for several hours, and Captain Brownell visited the Hebe. He returned just before night. A fair wind setting in from the eastward, we all stood in, the J. B. Gager, as being best acquainted with the navigation, taking the lead. The three vessels anchored about midnight, within twelve miles of the first narrows.

The next morning, it being calm, some of our men went on shore in the small boat, for a gunning excursion. They returned early in the forenoon, with a large number of sea-fowl. Not long after, Captain Brownell announced his intention to go ashore, and commenced making preparations. He soon changed his mind, however, and asked me to go, in his stead, to procure some fresh provisions, if they were to be had. Knowing, from the reports of whalers and others, something of the savage character of the natives, I felt reluctant to venture; but afterwards, to oblige the captain, I complied.

Taking our guns, a bag of bread, and some tobacco, four of us started for the shore. As we approached the beach, a crowd of black-looking giants came to the water's edge to gaze at us. We did not particularly fancy their looks, and lay on our oars for a considerable length of time. A recollection of the many ugly stories current about the Patagonians, their barbarous and cruel character, did not greatly fortify our confidence, or make us especially anxious for a personal acquaintance with them. We accordingly lay off in our boat, and, hailing them in Spanish, asked them if they had eggs, fowls, and beef. They replied, in broken Spanish, that they had plenty at their houses. I told them to produce their stores, and they should have plenty of bread in exchange. We parleyed with them for some time, till our boat at length touched the shore. I stood in the boat's stern, gun in hand, endeavoring to keep the natives from stealing, and warned the men not to leave the boat. They jumped ashore, promising not to stray from the spot. The Indians offered some skins for sale, which I paid for in bread. While my attention was diverted from them by this barter, the Indians were coaxing my men away. I looked about, and found only one man near me. He was despatched in pursuit of the others, and directed to bring them without delay. The tide at this point rises and falls forty-two feet. It was now ebb tide, the boat was fast grounding, and, it being large and heavily loaded, I was unable to get it off. The old chief and several other Indians crowded into it, and once in could not be got out. Persuasion was useless, and they were too many to be driven. In short, I was in their hands, and became immediately conscious of the difficulty and peril of my situation;—my men gone, I knew not where, the boat fast aground and crowded with the savages, while nearly a thousand of the tribe congregated upon the beach. What was before me, at the worst, I could only conjecture from report; and nothing but evil was reported of the creatures that surrounded me. What could I do? A question easier asked than answered.

After a long time, or what seemed such under circumstances that made minutes seem ages, one of my men came down, and asked permission to go to the Indian village, "a little way back from the shore," as they had been promised meat, eggs, and fowls. I ordered him to come immediately back to the boat. He persisted in urging his request, but it was so dangerously absurd that I absolutely refused. He then said he would inform his comrades of my refusal, and return immediately to the boat; but, for some cause, they seemed in no hurry to obey orders. Weary of waiting for them, and not without apprehension, I asked an Indian for the use of his horse, and rode with all speed after the fugitives. In the hurry of pursuit I inadvertently passed them, and tried to turn back my steed; but his inclinations were decidedly against a retreat. While our opposing impulses kept us stationary for a moment, I descried my men approaching on horseback, behind the Indians. When they came up I urged them to return to the boat. They persisted in going with the savages. I remonstrated with them on the impropriety and danger of their course, but in vain. Their mouths watered for the meat and eggs they were told of. Their cunning guides had completely allayed suspicion, and even laid to sleep their common prudence. The Indians kept on their course,—the men followed, and I felt at my wits' end. I rode from one to another, talking as industriously and as urgently as I could. At last I gave them peremptory orders to return. The Indians had plainly lied to us. Their village, they said, was only a little way off; and yet we were three-fourths of a mile from the boat, and not a house was yet in sight. Determined to go back, if I had to go alone, I turned my horse's head.

At this point the mask was thrown off. The Indians seized my bridle, and arrested my progress. We all dismounted, with a view to retreat on foot, but before I could reach the man nearest to me the Indians had robbed him of his gun. With a mutual agreement to stand by each other in case of pursuit, we hastened our retrograde march, but had made no great distance when we saw the Indians coming after us. They rode in advance of us, halted in our front, and manoeuvred to cut off our retreat; but by various zigzag movements, or boldly turning their horses' heads, we made considerable progress. Our foes, however, knew what they were at; it was only a question of time with them. A sudden and decided movement indicated a crisis. I drew my pistols (a pair of single-barrelled ones), but before I had time to cock one I was jumped upon from behind by some half-dozen of these monsters. One of them grasping a pistol by the barrel, I pointed it to his head and pulled the trigger. It missed fire, and I thank God that it did! Its discharge would have certainly killed him, and would as certainly have been revenged upon my life, probably upon the lives of my comrades. This is easily felt and said now; but at the moment, when excited by the struggle for liberty, and, as I feared, for life, with such dreaded enemies and at such formidable odds, it was quite another matter.

The old chief now came up, took me firmly by the wrist, and said, "Usted no bono! usted habla varmano por me casa, mucho, mala hombre currarhae! mucho montaro hombre!"—by which specimen of choice Spanish he desired to inform me that we promised to go to their houses, and now would not go; that we were bad men and liars. His peculiarly thick and guttural pronunciation did not make the dialect more intelligible; but I was in a situation where criticism would have been rather out of place, and my ears were quickened by the revelations made to sight. I therefore promptly replied, that if he would restrain his men from violence, we would go where he pleased. They, meanwhile, grasped their knives, and looked as if they wanted to use them on our persons; but the chief told them, No, not then; he would get rum and tobacco for us first, and kill us afterwards. Whilst I was thus engaged, my nearest companion discovered his gun in the hands of an Indian who stood not far from where I was struggling. Rushing suddenly upon him, he succeeded in recovering his piece,—more by tact than force, for his antagonist, like all the Patagonians, was very large and muscular. Then nimbly jumping aside, he told me to look out for myself. That was rather more than I felt able to do just at the moment. One Indian seized me by my arms and legs, some of them grasped my body, and others were busy investigating the contents of my pockets, and appropriating the same to their own use. And if he supposed himself able to show as much independence as he recommended me to, he was evidently mistaken. He had not elevated his gun to his face when the Indians were upon him, and wrenched it from his grasp. The old chief, all this time, held me tightly by the wrist, menacing his followers with his half-drawn cutlass, while I endeavored to bid for life and liberty. I told him he should have plenty of rum, tobacco, bread, flour, brass and beads, if he would carry us to the boat. At length he beat off my plunderers, and seemed on the point of yielding to my terms. He mounted his horse, and ordered me to get up behind him. I obeyed with alacrity, and fancied myself in a fair way to get out of trouble.

But, whatever may have been the chief's original intention, I had not gone far before his policy was diverted. One of the most audacious of the troop rode up, and insisted that I should not be allowed to return. I was the captain of the ship, he affirmed, and if I were restored they would get none of the promised rum and tobacco. The old savage seemed struck by this new suggestion, and halted. We then dismounted, and he led the horse up the hill, ordering me to follow. I was next directed to sit on the ground and wait further action. There I sat, looking alternately, with longing eyes, at the boat, and at our vessel riding at anchor in plain view. My three companions were soon brought to the spot, and dismounted. And now began a more earnest negotiation. We offered large ransom, and after some higgling they agreed that three of our number might be released, but one must remain as a hostage; and I was pointed out as the one. I endeavored to have one of the others stay, and one actually agreed to; but his heart soon failed him, and I could see that he was using all his powers of persuasion to provide for himself. I assured him that I would use every effort in his behalf, if he would consent to remain for the present; but he evidently thought of the maxim, "A bird in the hand," &c., and was bent on making sure of his own safety first of all. Poor fellow! I cannot blame him for loving his own life, though, at the moment, it did seem rather hard that, after getting into the scrape by their own headstrong folly, against my entreaties and peremptory commands, they should extricate themselves from it at my expense, and leave me to bear the hardest of it! Very likely I might have done the same, if our cases had been reversed. And, even if one of them had offered to remain, it is very doubtful whether the substitution would have been permitted. The Indians too evidently regarded me as the chief prize, and were bent on retaining me as such. They insisted that I must stay while the other three should go for ransom, and I had nothing to do but to submit.

Three Indians each took a man with him on a horse, and started for the boat. I watched them as they went, with feelings that I will not attempt to describe. It seemed but too probable we should never meet again. A sense of desolation came over me, at the thought of being left alone in the power of these savages, of whose treachery and cunning I had already had such ample experience, and of whose cruelty I had heard so much. I felt that I was beyond the aid, if not cut off from the sympathy, of my associates. The falseness of the Indians to all their engagements, as I afterwards learned, was signally displayed towards my more fortunate comrades. They evidently had no intention of releasing any of us. Before reaching the boat, they halted, and refused to go any further, or allow our men to leave them. The prisoners, however, struggled desperately, and at length got clear of their captors. One rushed up to his neck in water, the others sprang into the boat, pushed off, and rescued him as he was struggling with the waves. They reached the schooner, told their tale, and represented my desperate situation. All hands commenced breaking up cargo, to get at the rum and tobacco for my ransom. Two boats were forthwith manned, provided with the required articles, and with plenty of arms and ammunition, and started for the shore. They got to the land a little before dark, and pulled into a cove, or slight indentation of the beach.

On catching sight of them, I desired the Indians to conduct me to the shore, and receive the ransom. But this they declined. They ordered me to the summit of an eminence near by, there to beckon the men to come ashore. An old skin was given me to wave as a signal. Perceiving that I was to be used as a decoy to lure the others into their treacherous snare, and secure them all as prisoners, I protested against this new breach of faith, and assured them that our men would not leave their boat, but that, if they wanted any rum and tobacco, they must take me to the shore. To this, after a long palaver, and with visible reluctance, they assented. The old chief ordered me to mount his horse,—this time reversing our relative positions; he made me sit on the rude apology for a saddle and guide the horse, while he took his seat behind, clasping both arms tightly around my body, and spurring his old nag forward. Thus mounted, and wondering what would be the next trick of the savages, I was conveyed to the shore, near the spot where the boats lay off on their oars. Driving as near them as possible, I hailed the men,—told them by no means to fire on the Indians, but to give them all they had promised. They asked what they should do with the articles. I turned to the chief, told him what the boats had brought, and once more asked if it was a satisfactory ransom. He said, Yes; if those articles were laid down, I should be released. But he was plainly resolved to have his pay in advance; he distrusted us too much to let me go first; and I need not say that my confidence in him was far from implicit. But, "Nothing venture, nothing have,"—I directed the men to put the things ashore, which they did. The Indians greedily picked them up, and I claimed my release. The old rascal said, "he had not got plenty of rum yet, he must have a barrel." I insisted and struggled, but to no purpose. He kept a tight hold of my body, and when I begged that at least he would not squeeze me quite so painfully, he only redoubled his clasp. He obviously suspected, and I more than suspected, that it would not require a very great relaxation of his embrace to prompt a pretty decided movement on my part, for the effectual resisting of which the vicinity of the water was not altogether favorable. He now began spurring his old horse from the scene of action; I drew upon the bridle with my whole available force and weight; but the disparity between human strength and horse power, stimulated to its utmost by the spur, was too great. I begged the men in the boats to come again the next morning, and on no account to leave me, which they solemnly promised.

I was now hurried back into the country five or six miles, and at last reached an Indian village, and was set down by the old chief at his wigwam. He gave me in charge to one of his squaws, who ordered me into the hut and bade me sit down on the ground. While sitting there, and casting an inquisitive glance around the rude habitation, my attention was suddenly attracted to what appeared to be several pairs of eyes in a dark corner, shining with a strange brilliancy. I speculated silently on the sight, much doubting whether they belonged to human beings or to wild beasts; but, on carefully reconnoitring, I discovered that they belonged to three huge women. Further investigations disclosed a number of dark-skinned boys and girls, of divers ages and sizes, playing and capering about the premises, in a state of perfect nudity. It took a considerable time to make out these, or any other objects, distinctly, owing to the darkness of the hut. Presently the chief, the patriarch of the tribe, entered his habitation, and began a conversation, in his peculiar dialect, with his wives. He spoke in a low, guttural tone, in words the purport of which I could not gather. I was in no mood for conversation, but would have been much gratified by learning his version of the day's "stroke of business."

And now a few dry sticks and a bunch of dry grass were brought, mine host drew from a convenient repository a brass tinder-box, with a stone and a piece of steel, and soon produced a blaze that brilliantly illuminated the scene. By its light I was enabled to survey the first specimen of Patagonian architecture that had blessed my vision. It was constructed in a pointed style, though not very aspiring, consisting of a row of stakes about eight feet high, each terminating at top in a crotch, or fork, with a pole laid across them; two parallel rows of stakes on either side, about two feet high, with similar terminations, and a similar horizontal fixture; and a covering composed of skins of the guanaco, sewed together with the sinews of the ostrich, the only thread used by the people. This covering is drawn over the frame-work, and fastened by stakes driven through it into the ground. For purposes of ventilation some interstices are left, but these again are half closed by skins attached to the outside; so that the air from without, and the smoke from within (in default of a chimney), must insinuate themselves through these apertures in great moderation. In truth, my first survey was rather hurried; the first cheerful gleam had scarcely set my eyes on the look-out when I was fain to shut them against an intolerable smoke. In no long time I felt as bacon, if conscious, might be supposed to feel in the process of curing. No lapse of time was sufficient to reconcile my eyes, nostrils and lungs, to the nuisance; often have I been more than half strangled by it, and compelled to lie with my face to the ground, as the only endurable position. Talk that is "worse than a smoky house" must be something out of date, or Shakspeare's imagination never comprehended anything so detestable as a Patagonian hut. The chief and his numerous household, however, seemed to enjoy immense satisfaction; and jabbered and grunted, and played their antics, and exchanged grimaces, as complacently as if they breathed a highly exhilarating atmosphere.

My meditations and observations were shortly interrupted by preparations for a meal. The chief's better half—or rather fifth part, for he had four wives—superintended the culinary operations, which were as rude and simple as the hut where they were carried on. And now my fancy began to conjure up visions of the beef, fowls and eggs, the promise of which had lured my men from the boat,—had proved stronger than the suggestions of prudence, and had made me a prisoner. But these dainties, if they existed anywhere within the chief's jurisdiction, were just at present reserved. The old hag threw down from the top of one of the stakes that supported the tent the quarter of some animal; whether dog, guanaco, or whatever, was past imagining. She slashed right and left, with might and main, an old copper knife, till it was divided into several pieces. Then taking a number of crotched sticks, about two feet long, and sharpened at all their points, she inserted the forked ends into pieces of the meat, and drove the opposite points into the ground near the fire; which, though sufficient to smoke and comfortably warm the mess, was too feeble to roast it. At all events, time was too precious, or their unsophisticated appetites were too craving, to wait for such an operation; and the raw morsels were quickly snatched from the smoke, torn into bits by her dirty hands, and thrown upon the ground before us. The Indians seized them with avidity, and tossed a bit to me; but what could I do with it? I should have had no appetite for the dinner of an alderman at such a time and place; but as for tasting meat that came in such a questionable shape, there was no bringing my teeth or resolution to it. While eying it with ill-suppressed disgust, I observed the savages, like a horde of half-starved dogs, devouring their portions with the greatest relish; seizing the fragments with their fine white teeth, at the same time clenching them with their hands, and giving every sign of enjoyment except what one is accustomed to see in human beings. The old chief remarked the slight I was putting upon his hospitality, and broke in upon me with a fierce Por que usted, no munge usted, usted carna? Esta carna mucho bueno hombre por munge, se hombre, munge! "Why don't you eat your meat? This meat very good to eat,—very good to eat. Eat, man! eat!" I may here observe that my knowledge of Spanish, like the chief's, was colloquial; picked up here and there in voyages to South American ports, which may account for my orthography being so plainly determined by the ear rather than by any rules of Castilian grammar. Seeing him so much excited, and not knowing what deeds might follow his words if I refused, I thought it expedient to try to "eat what was set before me, asking no questions;" thinking, moreover, that if there were any evil spirit in it that the fire had failed to expel, it could not possibly have resisted the smoke. So, being sorely divided between aversion to the "strange flesh" and fear of showing it, I forced a morsel into my mouth. Its taste was by no means as offensive as its appearance had been unpromising, and I managed to save appearances with less disgust than I had feared. This was my first meal with the savages, and a sample of many others; though better viands afterwards varied their monotony, now and then.

The eating being over, a large horn, that had once adorned the head of a Spanish bullock, was dipped into a leathern bucket and passed from one to another. Between the bucket and the horn, the fluid had gained a flavor not found by Adam in his first brewing, and, indeed, not far from nauseating. However, it seemed expedient to "conquer my prejudices" so far as to drink with the other guests, and the ceremonies of dinner were over; for which, "with all other mercies," I felt thankful, and turned to my corner near the expiring fire, to chew the cud of sweet and bitter fancies, in which the latter ingredient decidedly predominated. The strange and sudden desolateness of my condition, the doubtful chances of escape, the possible sufferings before me, the uncertainty that rested on the designs of my savage captors, all rushed upon my mind, and suggested to my heated imagination a host of terrors.

These painful thoughts were interrupted by an order to prepare for the night's repose. An old skin, about two and a half feet square, was thrown upon the cold ground in the back part of our rookery, and assigned for my couch; I took possession accordingly, and the whole family bestowed themselves in a row near me. The stifling atmosphere was soon vocal with their snoring. My brain was too busy for sleep. Feverish fancies kept me wakeful. I revolved a variety of plans for escape. Could I steal out of the hut unperceived? Could I find my way to the shore? I doubted the first, and more than doubted the second; and even if so far successful, there was no boat to take me from the accursed land. And how could I conceal myself from the Indians till a boat should arrive? They would miss me; and, long before any possible communication with my vessel, would be hunting me down with horses and dogs. Not a wood or thicket had met my eye on the dreary waste I traversed the day before. I tried to devise some other plan, but none offered itself. It was this or nothing,—and this was next to nothing. Grown desperate, at last, I determined to make an effort.

After lying some time, listening to the heavy breathing of the sleepers, and satisfying myself that none of the company were awake, I raised myself as noiselessly as possible, and stole towards the front of the wigwam. Casting a furtive glance backward, I could see that the old chief was restless; either he had feigned sleep, or some evil spirit had waked him just at the wrong time. To go immediately back would too plainly betray my purpose; so I walked very calmly and deliberately into the open air, and stood as if star-gazing; the old fellow, as I plainly perceived, all the time watching me from the lodge. In a short time I walked quietly back to my dark retreat, and found him where I had left him, lying very coseyly, as if nothing had happened to disturb his slumbers. Once more stretching myself on my uneasy couch, I lay two hours or more, still revolving the same unsolved problem in my mind. At length, all appearing to be sound asleep, I decided to venture a second attempt; and, in the event of failure, to make the best of it for the present. Stealthily as possible I crawled from among them, slid out of doors, and crouched upon the grass. Could I be mistaken? No—those infernal eyes were fastened on me as before! There was no eluding their vigilance. At this moment a howling as of a hundred wolves was heard approaching, and about that number of dogs came rushing, pell-mell, towards me. I scampered for the wigwam as fast as my feet could carry me, and in my flight stumbled over a stick nearly eight feet long. I seized the weapon thus kindly lent me, and, swinging it furiously about me, gave all intruders that came within my reach a sufficient touch of its quality. Thus defending myself from the brutes, I backed towards the lodge, glad to shelter myself among its detested inmates. The cunning old Parosilver, as before, had bestowed himself on the ground among his squaws and dirty children, and was, apparently, fast asleep.

This was more than I could compass. Vexation at my fruitless attempts to escape,—dread, inspired by the relentless vigilance and quiet assurance of the chief,—tormenting apprehensions as to the issue of any effort on the morrow to effect my ransom,—all kept my brain upon the rack, and effectually drove sleep from my eyes, till near daylight, when I fell into a disturbed slumber. In my dreams I was at once transported from the savage hut, on board my vessel. Methought she was driving before the wind, all sails set, at full speed, upon a dangerous reef. All on board seemed insensible of the danger; I alone perceived it, but a nightmare spell was on me, and my lips refused to speak, my limbs to move. Rooted to my place on the deck, I stood in dumb agony, while our vessel rushed upon her fate. There came a sudden shock,—our bark had struck, and her total destruction was inevitable. Some of the men were dashed violently upon the deck, others precipitated into the boiling surf, where they clung desperately to spars, and fragments of the wreck. While the confusion was wildest, and the dream of effort for escape was subsiding into the calmness of despair, I suddenly awoke, and for some time was unable to comprehend where I was, or how I came there. If I were indeed shipwrecked, I was also, like Jonah, vomited upon dry land. I drew my hand across my eyes to assure myself that vision was unobstructed, cast my eyes right and left;—the lodge, the ashes of the last night's fire, the chief and his motley family, the door through which the "lubber fiend" had followed me with his restless eyes, and into which the fierce dogs had driven me, recalled my distracted senses, and restored consciousness of a reality which, at the moment, I would almost have exchanged for the wildest terrors of my dream.

With the light calmer thoughts succeeded, and I once more addressed myself to the task of effecting my escape. The first thing was to get the chief with me to the shore, in readiness to meet a boat, and to renew negotiations for my liberty. Observing that he was awake, I began to promise him an abundant supply of the articles most tempting to his fancy, on condition of my release. He carelessly replied that he would go with me to the beach by and by. I tried to urge his departure, being anxious to go without the rabble at his heels the day before, but for whose violence he would now hardly be master of me; but there was no hurrying his movements. He took down his little cutlass, drew it from its brazen scabbard, and commenced sharpening it with a rusty file, trying its edge with his fingers as the work went on, and casting side glances at me the while. Whether this ceremony was the preface to some act of violence he meditated, or a scene for effect, to fill me with a wholesome dread of his power, I could not guess; but, determined to show no foolish fears, I thought it best to put a bold face upon the matter, and make an equally striking demonstration of courage and presence of mind, qualities which savages generally appreciate. I therefore approached him, tried the edge with my own fingers, praised the beauty of the instrument, and interested myself in the process of sharpening it. Following up my assault on his vanity, I extolled him as one of the best of men, and assured him that when we got to the shore I would amply reward him for his kindness to me; taking occasion, however, to throw in a hint on the vast importance of starting early. This I enforced by the suggestion that, when he got his good things, the fewer there were present, the fewer claimants there would be to divide the spoils.

After much coaxing, he started after his old horse; I mounted behind him, and we moved slowly off. When we arrived at the shore it was blowing a perfect gale. A boat could not live in the billows. All three vessels had dragged their anchors, and lay at some distance from their anchorage of yesterday. Bark Hebe appeared to be dragging towards the Orange Bank, a dangerous shoal. I afterwards learned that the Hebe, after getting into water as shoal as would barely float her, slipped her cables, put up a little sail, and finally succeeded in weathering the shoal and getting safely out to sea. The J. B. Gager was dragging in the same direction. My own vessel was holding on better than the others, and I hoped she would ride out the gale in safety.

I made my captors understand the reason why no boat had come, as promised; with which they appeared to be satisfied, and we returned as we came. By means of their broken Spanish, which they had picked up from sailors, and in visits to the Chilian or other Spanish American settlements, and by signs, amounting at times pretty nearly to a pantomime, I found myself able to understand inquiries or commands, and to make known my wishes.

Early on the following morning we again visited the shore, and I looked eagerly toward the anchorage, where all my hopes of deliverance centred. Not a vessel was in sight! Whether they had foundered, or were driven upon the shoal and wrecked, or had dragged out to sea in a disabled condition,—or whether my shipmates, the gale having subsided, had deliberately proceeded on their voyage, and left me a prey to cruel savages and all the ills of this inhospitable shore,—I was unable to conjecture. I only knew that they were gone, and that I was left alone to the tender mercies of the Patagonians. No present means of escape appeared. The future, wisely hidden from my view, suggested none to my imagination. I told my captors the worst; that the high winds had probably sunk the ships, and all that were in them. At this intelligence they seemed delighted, and laughed immoderately, as if such a calamity were a consolation for the loss of their expected ransom. Their cruel glee could add nothing to the weight of my desolation. My past life was sealed up as if by an entrance on a new state of being. I looked round on a bleak and cheerless region, and forward on a life as barren of human joy, made up of every species of suffering,—hunger, cold, fatigue, insult, torture,—liable to be cut short at any moment by the caprice of my tormentors, and so wretched that death itself, with all the enormities of cannibalism, lost its terrors by comparison. Life, for any good or great purposes to be achieved, was over. And then my thoughts turned to far different scenes,—to happy faces, and pleasant voices, and familiar sights;—to hearts that beat with no dread of this day's calamities, felt no consciousness kindred to my despair, but would, in due time, be rudely awakened from their security. GOD help me, for I am helpless now!

CHAPTER II

A proposal to go to Port Famine negatived—"Holland"—Discovery of vessels in the straits—Double disappointment—A crisis—Survey of Patagonia—Scanty vegetation—Animals and birds—Climate— The people—Their habits and character—Domestic relations—Weapons—Government— Superstition—Cannibalism—Their reputation abroad.

Returning to the encampment, it remained to devise some new way of escape. Some four or five days' ride to the westward would bring us to Port Famine, on the straits, a penal settlement of Chili, and the only settlement in the vicinity by which I could hope to reënter the civilized world. A journey thither was suggested to the Indians, as the most likely way of turning my captivity to profitable account; but they refused with a promptness and decisiveness which was rather unaccountable, till I afterwards learned that they had lately visited that part of the country on a horse-stealing expedition, in which their success had been too good to make them desirous of showing their faces there at present. Money, guns, pistols, cutlasses, brass, beads, and everything else that could be thought of to tempt their cupidity, were offered. I was not disposed to be niggard of promises; but in vain. To Port Famine they were determined not to go; but old Parosilver assured me, by way of compensation, that he would take me to "Holland," which was a "much better place." Whereabout on terra firma this South American Holland was situated,—if, indeed, there was any such place, and the chief was not indulging in a little extra lying,— was past all conjecture. I inquired the distance. He could not tell exactly. Was it inhabited by Americans or English? There were "twenty or thirty white men there, and plenty of rum and tobacco." They promised to start with me towards Holland the next day. In what direction? They pointed towards the Atlantic. Well, I cared little where it was, or who lived there, provided only they were not Patagonians, and I could once get free of these rascals. But on the following morning the migration was postponed, in consequence of unexpected tidings.

One of the tribe, who had been down to the shore, reported that my vessel had come back. This welcome, though rather improbable information, started me, with about a dozen of them, on the track of his story. On gaining a view of the straits, a vessel was plainly in sight, but it was a strange sail. Yet, if I could succeed in boarding her, my purposes would be answered. She came into the bight of the bay, and anchored about fifteen miles below us. I endeavored to make my smutty companions comprehend that as the tide was then running out they would not make the shore till it turned, which would not be till night. They waited till near night, when hunger and thirst wore out their patience, and they ordered me off with them. Against this untimely mandate I warmly remonstrated, and after some dispute it was arranged that the chief should stay with me for the night. The rest returned to their encampment, and we made a good fire, which was kept up till nearly morning. Old Parosilver lay down under the lee of a clump of bushes, while I was busy in active exercise to keep warm, and replenishing the fire with dry bushes. At dusk I had observed the vessel hoisting sail, and beating up the bay. On this I began brandishing firebrands to attract notice, and walked to and fro on the beach for hours. The craft gradually approached, till her white canvas became distinguishable through the surrounding gloom. Fresh fuel was heaped on the fire, a bright blaze ascended; I took my station directly in front of it, holding out my coat, and frequently turning round, that my form and features might be more distinctly revealed. And now a thrill of joy electrified me, as I saw a light set on deck, which appeared to be stationary. There could be no doubt that the vessel had come to anchor directly opposite to us. Though hungry and weary with long watching, I hurried about, and gathered sticks and leaves in abundance to kindle a still brighter beacon-fire, in whose light and warmth anxiety began to expand into hope. At dawn of day, as the horizon lighted up, I could distinguish the vessel lying about a mile off, quiet as a sea-fowl on the calm surface. Presently there was a movement on deck, the anchor was hove up, the fore and main sails were hoisted, and the object on which my hopes and ardent prayers had centred through the cold night receded from view through the straits, bound, doubtless, for California. I watched the fast-vanishing sail with tearful eyes; and the old chief, who had been on the look-out, started for his horse, that had been hampered and turned out to crop among the scanty vegetation.

Before I had time to recover from the first revulsion of disappointment and grief, another vessel, a topsail schooner, came in by Point Dungeness. "Cheer up," I said to myself; "the sun will be shining, the darkness have given place to the clear day, before this vessel can be up and opposite to us." Confident of being noticed, I began active preparations for the approaching visitor. No rod of sufficient length was to be found; but, after some search, a number of short crooked sticks were collected. To lash them together, I tore up my drawers, which I could ill afford, and appropriated my shoe-strings. My flannel shirt was hoisted as a flag; and having replenished the fire, I paced the beach with colors flying, but, as the vessel approached, with increasing faintness of heart; for the wind gradually shifted, so that she could only take advantage of it by heading towards Terra del Fuego. At last she came opposite, but so near the further shore that the chances of success diminished every moment. Dark objects moved on the deck,—fancy painted them as men;—would they not discover me through their glasses, and be drawn by my signal of distress? No; onward she floated away,—the narrows were soon passed, and my vision of deliverance was dissipated.

With this final death-blow to all present hopes of relief, I turned away in despair. Exhausted by hunger, cold and fatigue, and worn out by hours of anxiety, I fell helpless upon the ground, and wept like a child. For the first time I felt utterly forsaken, and repined at my lot as one of unmitigated evil. Effort seemed useless; I had neither resolution nor strength to make further exertion. There was nothing for me but listless endurance. I even reproached myself that I had not cast myself into the sea, and staked my life on the chance of swimming to the schooner. There was no possibility of doing this; but failure would have been only death, and what was life worth to me here? This tempest of self-reproach soon spent itself. My temperament is too buoyant to be long depressed, and calm and stout thoughts took the place of despairing weakness. It was unmanly, something whispered within me, thus to give way before difficulties. It would be time enough to do this when all possible effort had failed. The weak and imbecile might take refuge in despair, but the strength of youth should serve me better. I called to mind examples of courage in greater emergencies, when obstacles that seemed insurmountable had been conquered by fortitude and perseverance. "Heaven helps those who help themselves." The more I reflected on the matter, the stronger grew the impulses of faith and courage, by whose force it seemed possible to win a triumph against the greatest odds. Before rising from the earth, my resolution was fully taken to throw discouragement to the winds; by the help of God to meet whatever impended with the courage of a man; to bear my calamities with patient endurance; and to give up hope and energy only when nothing was left to be attempted, or the power to do and suffer was exhausted.

I rose a new man,—my strength invigorated, my soul fortified by a strong purpose. Though the cold night air had thoroughly chilled my frame, it now felt a warmth kindled by the fires within, and an unaccustomed flush suffused my countenance. The resolve fixed in this memorable crisis of my captivity, though severely tested, was never wholly overborne. Henceforth, the events and scenes through which I passed were viewed with a calmness that had been before unattainable, and which is now scarcely credible, on recollection. So true is it that our strength is unknown to ourselves till it is thoroughly tested.

The hope of immediate release, however, was at an end; my savage captors, it seemed, must be looked upon as for an indefinite period my masters and companions; and I had nothing at present to do but to divert myself by a study of their manners and habits; to consult my safety by a close study of their character, and of the ways and means by which so to adapt my deportment to it as to win their confidence, to disarm hostility, and to seize opportunities.

Patagonia, as it offered itself to my observation, more than answered the descriptions of geographers,—bleak, barren, desolate, beyond description or conception,—only to be appreciated by being seen. Viewed from the Straits of Magellan, it rises in gentle undulations or terraces. Far as the eye can reach, in a westerly direction, it assumes a more broken and hilly appearance, and long ranges of mountains, extending from north to south, divide the eastern from the western shore. The soil is of a light, sandy character, and bears nothing worthy the name of a tree. Low bushes, or underwood, are tolerably abundant, and in the valleys a coarse, wiry grass grows luxuriantly. Streams of water are rare. The natives draw their supplies principally from springs or pools in the valleys, the water of which is generally brackish and disagreeable.

The variety of animal is nearly as limited as that of vegetable productions. The guanaco, a quadruped allied to the lama, and with some resemblance to the camelopard, is found in considerable numbers. It is larger than the red deer, fleet on the foot, usually found in large herds, frequenting not only the plains, but found along the course of the Andes. Its flesh is a principal article of food; its skin is dried with the hair on, in such a manner that, when wet, it retains its pliability and softness. This process of preserving skins seems to be peculiar to the Indian tribes, and is not unlike that by which buffalo-robes, bear-skins, buckskins, and other articles of luxury, and even necessity, among us, are prepared by the North American Indians. Guanaco-skins are cut into pieces of all sizes, and sewed into a thousand fanciful patterns, every workman originating a style to suit himself. The hoofs are sometimes turned to account by the natives as soles for shoes, when they indulge in such a luxury, which is not often.

The enemy of the guanaco is the cougar, or "American lion," smaller than its African namesake, and more resembling the tiger in his character and habits, having a smooth, sleek coat, of a brownish yellow color,—altogether a very beautiful but ferocious creature. His chase is a favorite, though rare and dangerous, sport of the natives. Patagonia likewise boasts of the skunk, whose flesh is used for food.

There are also foxes, and innumerable mice. Of birds, the only noticeable varieties are the condor, in the Andes, and the cassowary, a species of ostrich, smaller than that of Africa, on the plains; its plumage is not abundant, generally of a gray or dun color. Its flesh is tender and sweet, and with the fat much prized by the Indians. Like the African ostrich, it is exceedingly swift, only to be captured on horseback, and often fleet enough to outrun the fastest racer.

The climate is severe. The Rio Negro forms the northern boundary, and nearly the whole country is south of the parallel of 40° south latitude. At the time of my capture, which was in the month of May, the weather corresponded to that of November in the New England States. Its chilliness, however, was greatly increased by the bleak winds of that exposed locality. Along the Straits of Magellan the weather is also exceedingly changeable. Sudden and severe squalls, often amounting almost to a hurricane, vex the navigation of the straits, and sweep over the coast with fearful fury.

The habits of the Patagonians, or at least of the tribe among whom I was cast, are migratory, wandering over the country in quest of game, or as their caprice may prompt them. They subsist altogether on the flesh of animals and birds. The guanaco furnishes most of their food, and all their clothing. A mantle of skins, sewed with the sinews of the ostrich, fitting closely about the neck and extending below the knee, is their only article of dress, except in the coldest weather, when a kind of shoe, made of the hind hoof and a portion of the skin above it, serves to protect their inferior extremities.

In person they are large; on first sight, they appear absolutely gigantic. They are taller than any other race I have seen, though it is impossible to give any accurate description. The only standard of measurement I had was my own height, which is about five feet ten inches. I could stand very easily under the arms of many of them, and all the men were at least a head taller than myself. Their average height, I should think, is nearly six and a half feet, and there were specimens that could have been little less than seven feet high. They have broad shoulders, full and well-developed chests, frames muscular and finely proportioned, the whole figure and air making an impression like that which the first view of the sons of Anak is recorded to have made on the children of Israel. They exhibit enormous strength, whenever they are sufficiently aroused to shake off their constitutional laziness and exert it. They have large heads, high cheek-bones, like the North American Indians, whom they also resemble in their complexion, though it is a shade or two darker. Their foreheads are broad, but low, the hair covering them nearly to the eyes; eyes full, generally black, or of a dark brown, and brilliant, though expressive of but little intelligence. Thick, coarse, and stiff hair protects the head, its abundance making any artificial covering superfluous. It is worn long, generally divided at the neck, so as to hang in two folds over the shoulders and back, but is sometimes bound above the temples, by a fillet, over which it flows in ample luxuriance. Like more civilized people, the Patagonians take great pride in the proper disposition and effective display of their hair. Their teeth are really beautiful, sound and white,—about the only attractive and enviable feature of their persons. Feet and hands are large, but not disproportionate to their total bulk. They have deep, heavy voices, and speak in guttural tones,—the worst guttural I ever heard,—with a muttering, indistinct articulation, much as if their mouths were filled with hot pudding. Their countenances are generally stupid, but, on closer inspection, there is a gleam of low cunning that flashes through this dull mask, and is increasingly discernible on acquaintance with them; when excited, or engaged in any earnest business that calls their faculties into full exercise, their features light up with unexpected intelligence and animation. In fact, as one becomes familiar with them, he will not fail to detect an habitual expression of "secretiveness" and duplicity, which he will wonder he did not observe sooner. They are almost as imitative as monkeys, and are all great liars; falsehood is universal and inveterate with men, women and children. The youngest seem to inherit the taint, and vie with the oldest in displaying it. The detection of a falsehood gives them no shame or uneasiness. To these traits should be added a thorough-paced treachery, and, what might seem rather inconsistent with their other qualities, a large share of vanity, and an immoderate love of praise. They are excessively filthy in their personal habits. Hydrophobia, so to speak, is a prevailing distemper; they never wash themselves. Hands and faces are covered with dirt, so thick, and of such ancient deposit, that their natural color only appears in spots, laid bare by the mechanical loosening and displacement of some of the strata, which curiously variegates the surface. It is hardly necessary to remark that such a condition of the skin is highly favorable to the increase and multiplication of "the moving creature that hath life," wherewith their persons are abundantly peopled.

The women are proportionally smaller than the men, and rather inclined to embonpoint. The old chief had four wives, though he had probably never heard of Mahomet or his domestic laws. The rest of the tribe had only one wife apiece. The women erect the wigwams, provide fuel and cook,—if the operation should be dignified with that name,—in short, all the drudgery falls to their lot. They are treated as slaves, but made, in most respects, as comfortable in their servitude as the condition of their rude masters will admit. When, however, their lords are excited by gambling, or enraged for any or no cause, the fury of passion is visited upon their defenceless heads, which they bear uncomplainingly, with a meek submissiveness worthy of better treatment. They are passionately fond of trinkets and clumsy ornaments, such as bits of brass and copper, beads, and the like, which they wear suspended from their necks. A few of them had their ears pierced, and wore brass or copper ear-rings; and many of them decked out their children with similar rude finery, which is valued more than anything else, except rum, tobacco and bread. The men paint or bedaub their faces and breasts with a kind of red earth. Charcoal is also used as a cosmetic. A broad line of red alternating with a stripe of black, in various fantastic figures, is a favorite style of decoration. The women make themselves, if possible, still more hideous, by the application of a pigment made of clay, blood and grease. Some of them would be very comely, if only cleanly, and content to leave nature less strenuously adorned.

The people are as deficient in the morals as in the refinements and courtesies of domestic life; their licentiousness is equal to their cruelty,—the filth of their persons only too faithfully represents the degree in which "their mind and conscience is defiled." I saw no person, of either sex, that appeared to have attained advanced age, though it was difficult to judge of this. The oldest Indian I remember to have seen did not seem to be above sixty.

Their only wealth, aside from their huts, consists of horses, the stock of which is frequently replenished by stealing from the Spanish and Chilian settlements. These animals are, for the most part, of small size and inferior quality, half wild, coated with coarse, shaggy hair—lean and woe-begone enough, just "fit for the crows." A few valuable specimens of a superior breed are found among them, doubtless "conveyed" there. The rude saddles in use among them are mostly of Spanish origin, obtained at the settlements. They consist each of two boards, an inch thick, six inches wide, and two feet long, rounded at the corners so as to fit the horse's back, and united by two strips of board passing across the back-bone, the several pieces lashed together with leather strings. A piece of guanaco-skin often serves in default of a saddle. The steed is guided by a single rein, tied round the lower jaw; some of them sport a bit of iron or wood, secured by a string round the jaw, attaching the rein to this. Spurs, like the rest of their riding apparatus, are more efficient than elegant. They are indeed rude and cruel things,—straight sticks, six inches long, with a long, sharp iron inserted into the end, secured by a string or strap around the hollow of the foot, and tied at the top, a second strap nearer the heel, and a third passing round the heel. They are all agile and excellent horsemen.

For weapons, the chief, and a few of the principal men, had cutlasses or swords. They had no fire-arms, nor could I learn that they understood their use; bows and arrows, spears and war-clubs, appeared to be equally unknown. All the men carried knives; and the bolas, a missile weapon used in the capture of all kinds of game. This consists of two round stones, or lead balls, if they can be procured weighing each about a pound, connected by a strap or thong of leather, ten or twelve feet long. When engaged in the chase, his horse at his highest speed, the rider holds one ball in his hand, and whirls the other rapidly above his head; when it has acquired sufficient momentum it is hurled with unerring aim at the object of pursuit, and either strikes the victim dead, or coils inextricably about him and roots him to the spot, a helpless mark for the hunter's knife.

This tribe numbered about one thousand; the chief is the acknowledged head of the people. Whether his power was hereditary or elective, I could not learn; but incline to the belief that it was hereditary, as it appeared to be, in his theory at least, absolute. In all questions of importance his decision is final; yet his subjects take considerable liberty with his opinions, sometimes oppose his counsels, and even question his authority. On the appearance of such democratic symptoms, he sometimes finds it necessary to assert his sovereignty with spirit, and brandishes his cutlass smartly before their eyes.

The habits of the people are not only filthy, but indolent to the last degree; exertion of body or mind is their greatest dread. They never go on a hunting expedition till there is nothing more to eat, nor even then till they feel the spur of extreme hunger. It sometimes happens that at such a crisis a storm comes on, which shuts them in; and it is no unfrequent occurrence for them, under such circumstances, to pass two or three days without tasting food. They learn nothing by experience; the same childish indolence and recklessness, followed by the same painful consequences, are continually recurring.

Though their great size at first sight was fitted to inspire terror, it required no very long observation to discover that they were deficient in natural courage. This, in fact, might be inferred at once, from their habitual deceit, treachery and artifice, which are the defences of the weak and timorous, rather than the weapons of strong and daring natures. They always select the night to inflict injuries; never meet an enemy in open combat whom they can stab from behind, or despatch in the dark; and, when obliged to attack by day, always do so in large numbers. This defect of courage is increased by their superstition; they have great faith in charms, signs and omens, a weakness which I anticipated might exert great influence on my destiny in important conjunctures. Could I by any means so master their secret as to possess myself of its mystic power, it might prove an effective aid to my plans of self-defence, or of escape. Should it, on the other hand, be turned by any accidental causes against me, its impulse might prove irresistible by power or contrivance. There was no appearance of idolatrous worship among them, nor could I observe any allusion to a Supreme Being, or to any superior powers having personal attributes; and, except a single ceremony, of which more hereafter, the nature of which was and is still inexplicable, there was nothing that suggested to my mind the idea of religious worship. Whether they are cannibals or not, has been a matter of some dispute. So far as I know, they have been, heretofore, only casually observed on the beach by voyagers, or vaguely reported of by the people of adjoining countries and neighboring settlements; neither of which is a sufficiently reliable source of information. My own personal advantages on this head were greater; but I am obliged, after all, to leave the question about where I found it, so far as certain conclusions are concerned. Yet some circumstances occurred, or were related to me, that incline my mind strongly to the belief that such horrible practices are not unjustly ascribed to them. Of the soundness of my conclusions those who follow the course of the narrative will have the opportunity of judging for themselves; if such had been my persuasion at the beginning, it may be readily imagined what effect this last hazard would have had upon my feelings, in contemplating the possibilities of the future. Happily a convenient scepticism on this point preserved me from this dark apprehension.

I came among these people not, certainly, with the best preparation in my previous habits and associations to endure either the climate of the country or the hardships of captivity. I went on shore in my usual ship's dress; thick frock coat, trousers, and shoes, and glazed cap. My under-garments were woollen; though an important item, as before related, was made way with in fruitlessly signalling vessels in the straits. But to live without any change of dress, to sleep without any additional covering, protected from the cold ground only by a fragment of guanaco-hide, and the other discomforts and exposures of life among savages, made, altogether, a harsh contrast to the comforts of our good schooner. To these, however, I gradually became inured, till I was able to meet cold and wet and storm with as stoical indifference as my dark companions, who had known no other lot from infancy.

Of the character of the natives I had little previous knowledge; and that little was not adapted to stimulate curiosity, or prompt the least anxiety for more intimate acquaintance. It was derived mainly from whalers, in whom it seemed to have produced much the same degree of contentment,—a feeling that ignorance is bliss. Indeed, the greatest caution has always been employed by voyagers in regard to landing on these shores; many experienced seamen cannot be persuaded to land at all; trade with the natives is always carried on in boats off shore, frequently with loaded fire-arms constantly levelled, in readiness for action in case of emergency. But here I was, put forcibly to the study of their character in the school of dame Experience, and can testify to the truth of the saying that she charges roundly for tuition. Let the reader give me credit for the cheapness with which I put him in possession of what knowledge was purchased at so exorbitant a price.

CHAPTER III

Hard journey—Encampment—Division of the tribe—My new guardian—Story of the capture of a British vessel—Reünion—Gambling—Culinary arts—Hunting—Symptoms of danger—Mutual deceptions—Tough yarns—The fatal ring—An effective oration—Indecision of the Indians.

The reader left me just rising from a half-stupor into which a double disappointment had thrown me, feverish with the excitement of new purposes and resolutions. The first aim was for some fresh water, to allay a burning thirst. After a long and unsuccessful search, I went deliberately to the beach and took a deep draught of the briny waves. Expecting that the chief would shortly return for me with a train of his followers, it occurred to me that I might secrete myself, though there was nothing certain to be gained by it, if I were successful, of which the probability was not great. With this object in view, I walked along close on the water's edge, that my footprints might be obliterated by the waves. After proceeding in this way for some distance, I left the shore, and started towards the interior, in quest of a place where I might dig a hole in the earth and cover myself with grass and bushes. I had gone but a little way inland, when, on ascending a slight eminence, whom should I meet, face to face, but the old chief and another of my tormentors! So the scheme came to nothing; but after others more feasible had so dolefully miscarried, it was not in human nature to lay this disappointment very deeply to heart. I made as though I was glad to see the old fellow, though, could I then have had my will of the savages, they would have been safely anchored in the middle of the straits. I told him (Heaven forgive me!) I was looking for them. The chief responded to my greeting only by ordering me to mount his horse. I requested leave to stay a little longer, and was refused. I again requested to be taken to Port Famine;— no, I should be taken to "Holland."

I mounted behind him, and we travelled all day in the direction of Cape Virgin. For two days and nights I had eaten nothing, and drunk nothing but sea-water, and, in fact, had taken very little food for three days. We arrived about dark at an eminence commanding a view of their new squatting ground. Here we halted to take a short survey of the encampment. To them, doubtless, the prospect was beautiful; to me it was heart-sickening, but I strove to keep up cheerful appearances. Down in a valley or deep marshy hollow, covered with tall grass or rushes, an almost innumerable drove of horses were seen grazing; and beyond, at a short distance, the surface was thickly dotted with huts, erected, or in process of erection, by female architects. Children, in swarms like summer flies, and with no more artificial covering than those insects, were capering and shouting in high glee. At length we descended to the rude village; after tacking about, first to the right and then to the left, like a ship against a head wind, we came gallantly into town, and drew up at the chief's lodge. I was glad to dismount, sore with bestriding the skeleton of a horse.

Here I again took the liberty of proposing a trip to Port Famine, offering to go alone, if they would not go with me. The chief told me, with emphasis, to say no more about it. He would take me to "Holland," and there get rum and tobacco. "Only get me there," I said to myself, "and much good may your rum and tobacco do your old carcass!"

On the third day of our encampment here the tribe was divided, and I was sent off with one of the chief's lieutenants. A more blood-thirsty rascal could not be found in the tribe. This step was probably taken by the chief to get rid of my importunities to visit Port Famine, the frequent renewal of which had evidently worried him. My new guardian regaled my ears, from time to time, with stories of his murderous exploits, most likely in order to instil into me a wholesome dread of his power, and a submissive temper under his authority. The details of his bloody yarns are too shocking to repeat. One story, on which he seemed to dwell with peculiar satisfaction, as it was confirmed by more reliable authority afterwards, I will here relate, with such other particulars as I gained by subsequent information.

About two years before, the British brig Avon was in the Santa Cruz river. Captain Eaton, her commander, went on shore with his men, and bought some horses of the Indians, which he paid for in rum, tobacco and trinkets. After receiving their pay, they played the same trick as with me,—refused to deliver the horses. The captain was about getting under weigh, when the Indians, perceiving his intention to leave them, went down to the shore opposite the vessel, and beckoned him to come on shore, signifying that they would give up the horses, as agreed. The boat was sent ashore, and six or eight Indians returned in it to the brig. They surrounded the captain on the quarter-deck, and told him the horses were coming. He stepped to the rail with his glass, to observe motions on shore; while thus engaged, the savages came up behind, drew out their long knives, and stabbed him to the heart. He sunk lifeless on the rail, and fell upon the deck. Seizing him by the hair, and raising him partly on their knees, they cut his throat, and stabbed him again and again, to make the work of death sure. They then rushed upon the mate and stabbed him, but not mortally; he threw himself exhausted down the hatchway, and had just strength enough to secrete himself among the cargo. The boy was dealt with in the same manner as the captain, and one or two sailors, being wounded, succeeded, like the mate, in getting below deck and secreting themselves. The remainder of the crew were fortunately off in a boat at this time, and escaped the massacre. The savages ate and drank on board, and then plundered the brig of such articles as suited their fancy. Mr. Douglass, of "Holland," being on board the brig, was not murdered, but carried on shore and detained. A gentleman named Simms afterwards endeavored to effect the release of Mr. Douglass. He gave them all that they demanded as ransom, and was then himself detained to keep his friend company. A third embassy was undertaken by Mr. John Hall, of whom the reader will learn more hereafter. He paid a large ransom for his two friends, and was then served as they had been. He succeeded in effecting his escape the next day; but Douglass and Simms were carried off, murdered, and, it is supposed,—I believe with good reason,—that their bodies were eaten. The Avon, after being plundered, fell into the hands of the remainder of the crew, and sailed for Montevideo.

I travelled with this ruffian about ten days. He was a hard master, though I cannot charge him with personal ill-treatment that amounted to cruelty. Our life was monotonous enough. We slept a good share of the time when we rested, drank pure water when we could get it, and ate what fell in our way; though the reader may be assured that we saw some hungry days. At the expiration of ten days, the tribe was reünited at a place agreed upon. Here we continued several days, the natives occupied exclusively with gambling, which was alike their daily labor and recreation. When the demands of hunger became too imperative to be longer postponed, they would go out and hunt, after which they resumed their games.

Gambling is a vice to which they are greatly addicted, and they pursue it with a perseverance and ardor worthy of amateurs in more civilized communities. The implements used are bits of guanaco-skin, about the size of common playing-cards, on which are rudely depicted dogs and a variety of other beasts, with divers mystic marks and scrawls, done with a stick in a pigment composed of clay, blood and grease. Unlike their compeers in more enlightened circles, they put down stakes on only one side, for which the opposite players contend. In this way they rid themselves of their saddles, bridles, knives, and whatever other portable articles they may have to hazard. Nay, I have seen them inflamed to such a passion as to take the mantles from their women's shoulders, telling them to protect themselves from the cold as they could.

But where was "Holland," all this time? They told me at first that we should be only four days reaching it, and already more than ten had passed. On inquiry, they said that the journey would be completed in six days; on we went, for sixteen days more, with the same dull routine, the Indians assigning seven or eight days as the minimum time. The place seemed to be all the while receding. I had long since become aware that there was no truth in them; but persisted in questioning them, to call forth fresh lies, which they uttered with marvellous fluency, as if it were vastly easier than speaking the truth.

After the reünion of the tribe, I implored the old chief to take me back to his lodge, and to his especial care; to which he consented, much to my satisfaction. With him I felt a kind of security unknown elsewhere; under God, I relied alone on his protection. He alone of the tribe had the power to defend me, and I spared no pains to secure his good-will. To this end, I made him large promises of such things as I thought would arouse his cupidity, or stimulate his appetites, as well as an abundance of ornaments for his wives and children, if he would only take me to some place inhabited by white people. This policy was extended to his household; disagreeable as the task was, I forced myself to caress his dirty children, and to tell them what pretty things I intended to give them. By these, and such-like demonstrations, I flattered myself it might be possible to keep on peaceable terms with old Parosilver, and enlist his authority for me, if circumstances should compel me to appeal to it.

The reünited tribe remained in camp three or four days, dividing their time between gambling and hunting. When I accompanied the hunters, as I sometimes did, I was sure to get something to eat towards night, as they invariably kindled a fire and cooked part of the game on the spot where it was killed. Their method of preparing all meats was essentially the same as has been described; tossing large pieces into the fire, or suspending them over it, till they were somewhat smoked and dried, and then devouring them, without salt, or any other condiment but the sauce of hunger. Cooking the ostrich, however, forms an exception: the feathers are plucked out, the bones dissected and removed; hot stones are placed within the body, the skin is tightly sewed together, and the whole is partially roasted on the embers. The lacings are then cut, and the meat is served up; it has an excellent flavor, far surpassing that of the domestic turkey. The bird is covered with a layer of fat, half an inch thick, which is melted, and collects in the body, forming a condiment which is relished as the greatest luxury of Patagonian living. If any fragments of the repast remain, they are slung to the backs of the saddles, and so carried home, dangling at the horses' sides, till they are so begrimed with dust as to defy all conjecture as to their quality or origin. These choice morsels are proffered to the home department, are received with smiles of gratitude, and devoured with a gust sharpened by long abstinence. It was noticeable that the plumage of the ostrich, though beautiful, was not at all valued by the Indians; large quantities of the feathers are blown all over the country, without attracting the least regard, while men and women disfigure themselves with paint, and load their persons with the cheapest of all trumpery, brass and copper and beads, picked up from traders, or stolen.

The hunting of the guanaco is not only their chief reliance for food, but a spirited amusement, conducted after a fashion peculiar alike to hunters and hunted. Patagonia, as before mentioned, has no trees, but is covered here and there, in patches, with a kind of under-brush of scrub growth, and the plains extend back for hundreds of miles from the Atlantic shore, like a vast rolling prairie. This affords a clear and excellent hunting-ground, with nothing to conceal the game, or hinder the pursuer, except now and then a clump of low bushes, or the tall grass of the marshes. Two to four hundred Indians on horseback, bare-headed, and with their skin mantles about them, and each having the bolas and his long knife tucked beneath his belt, the whole followed by an innumerable pack of dogs of every kind, down to curs of low degree, make up a hunting party; as far as the eye can reach, their gigantic forms, diminished by the distance, may be seen projected on the horizon, their long hair streaming in the wind. Presently a thickness is perceived in the air, and a cloud of dust arises,—a sure indication that a herd of guanacos has been beaten up, and is now approaching. All eyes are fixed intently on the cloud; it soon appears as if several acres of earth were alive, and in rapid motion. There is a herd of from five hundred to a thousand of these animals, infuriated, rushing forward at their utmost speed whatever direction they may chance to take, they follow in a straight line; and, as soon as their course is ascertained, the Indians may be seen running their horses at break-neck pace to plant themselves directly in the course of the living tide. As the game approach, the hunter puts spurs to his horse and rushes across their track. When within twenty or thirty yards, he jerks the bolas from his girdle, and, whirling it violently above his head, lets fly. The weapon usually strikes the head or neck of the animal, and winds itself about his fore-legs, bringing him to the ground. The hunter dismounts, cuts the victim's throat, remounts, and is again in pursuit. The whizzing missile, unerring in its aim, brings down another and another, till the party are satisfied with their chase and their prey. The dogs fall upon the poor animals, when helplessly entangled by the bolas, and often cruelly mangle them before the hunter has time to despatch them. Seldom does any one miss the game he marks. It is the height of manly ambition among them, the last result of their training, to excel in the chase.

The sport being over, then comes the dressing of the meat. The body is split open, the entrails removed, the heart and large veins opened, to permit the blood to flow into the cavity. The Indians scoop up with their hands and eagerly drink the blood. When their thirst is satisfied, the remainder is poured into certain of the intestines selected for the purpose, to become (to their accommodating tastes) a luxury as highly prized as any surnamed of Bologna. The ribs are disjointed from the back-bone, and, with the head, discarded as worthless. The body is quartered, cutting through the skin; the quarters, tied together in pairs, are thrown across the horses' backs, and conveyed to the camp. Arrived at their wigwams, the chivalrous hunters never unlade their beasts, but lean upon the horses' necks till their wives come out and relieve them of the spoil. They then dismount, unsaddle their horses, and turn them loose.

Whilst remaining at our present encampment, strong indications of dissatisfaction were apparent, which manifestly had reference to me. There was a large party that had always entertained hostile feelings towards me; and I now found it necessary to exert myself to the utmost to quell their discontent, by making large promises of presents to men, women and children, "due and payable" on arrival at some white settlement; also, by humoring their caprices, and flattering their vanity with the most honeyed words at my command. The reader, I hope, will not harshly judge of the deceptions which are here and elsewhere avowed in this narrative. I was placed in circumstances which, it seemed to me, made this a legitimate and necessary mode of self-defence. It was plain that my only way of escape would be by some negotiation for ransom, and the Indians had conceived expectations of very large profit to be made out of me. They were told, when we landed, that I was the captain of the ship,—an unfortunate error, but one that I could not repair. I was naturally looked upon as so much the more valuable hostage. My only resource was to act in character: to magnify my own importance, to increase their expectations, whenever I found myself sinking in the scale of their favor,—to make them feel, in short, that they had an immense interest in preserving my life, and getting me to "Holland," or some other white settlement, with the most convenient speed. And if some of the fictions appear gross, it is enough to say that they were such as seemed, at the time, to be adapted to the grossness of their apprehensions and desires, and to the most sure accomplishment of the purpose in view.

Yet, so false-hearted and treacherous were they, that one could never be for a moment certain what impression was made. Liars in grain themselves, it was only natural for them to distrust every one else. Whenever I spoke, and especially when making promises, the old chief would look me steadily in the eye, as though piercing my inmost thoughts. But, in process of time, I so schooled myself to the exercise, that I could return his look and tell the toughest stories without blinking. Some of them were to the full as credible as those of Munchausen. It was constantly necessary to put memory and imagination to the rack, to call forth something new and astonishing wherewith to divert their fancy, and preöccupy their minds from meditating mischief against me, of which I had continual reason to be afraid. Secure against any detection of the plagiarism, I drew largely from the adventures of Sinbad the Sailor, the marvels of the Arabian Nights, and the cunning devices of Gil Blas, the materials of which served, when duly mixed with my own veritable experience, to excite their curiosity, if not to awaken awe and superstitious reverence. They would sit around me for hours, as eager as so many children, their eyes and ears all intent, while in broken Spanish, mixed with a few Indian phrases that had been grafted into my speech through the ear, aided by abundant gesticulations, that shadowed forth and illustrated whatever was obscure in expression, I spun yarns of no common length, strength and elasticity. Sometimes, in response to a general call from the company, the old chief at the end of some marvellous tale, would command me to tell it again. This was no easy task, considering the freaks which my imagination usually played, without restraint, in the progress of the narrative. In no long time, however, I learned to imitate the prudence of boys who turn down the leaves of their books, or of Indians who break down the shrubs and twigs along a new path, by taking special note of my deviations,—a sort of mental dog's-ear, or way-mark, interposed at the point of departure. It was not difficult to retrace the way at their bidding, and give them the whole journey, to its minutest turnings.

The excitement and dissatisfaction which I had remarked and dreaded appeared to have died away, when one night I had startling evidence that it was still active. At the usual hour of rest, as I was expecting every moment to be ordered, like a dog, to my cold corner of the lodge, a gigantic, ill-favored fellow made his appearance, and exchanged, in an under tone, a few words with the chief. Without comprehending a word that was passing, I could see, by their significant glances, that the colloquy concerned me, and that it boded me no good. The giant soon disappeared. The chief sat a moment in silence, rose, and ordered me to follow him. To the question where he was taking me, no other answer was vouchsafed than "Come along!" We had proceeded but a short distance when I observed a group of Indians sitting in a circle on the earth. The sight almost froze my blood. The most dismal apprehensions seized upon me. There needed no wizard to tell the import of the scene. The fatal ring, so much to be dreaded by those who are cast upon the tender mercies of savages, was set for me. The suddenness of it aggravated the blow. It almost paralyzed thought, and arrested my powers of motion. The catastrophe of the tragedy, I thought, is at hand, unless arrested by the interposition of a higher power. In my way to the dreaded spot I sent up a silent supplication that He whose eye marked all my footsteps, and whose power was all-sufficient for my protection against utmost peril, would keep me in that hour of my "extremity," and make it, according to the proverb, His "opportunity."

Arrived at the ring, I found the Indians squatting on the ice and snow awaiting us, with their cutlasses and large knives tucked under their blankets,—weapons they never carry except when they expect to use them. I was ordered within, and seated myself as near as possible to the chief. They presently began talking in rotation, as they sat, in their own tongue. Their words were mainly unintelligible; but the deadly malice that flashed from the eyes, kindled in the features, and animated the gesticulations, of some of them, left no room to doubt the significance of their speech. A part of them were clamorous against my life, as they had constantly been. Others appeared to be irresolute, and said little; but, so far as could be discovered, no voice was raised in my favor. The chief spoke last,—I hung upon his lips, and anxiously scrutinized his face and action. I gathered that he was in favor of holding on a while longer, and using me as a decoy, to lure others within their power; reminding them of my promises,—the quantities of rum and tobacco they were to get from me, the trinkets destined for women and children. He was for getting the booty before cutting the matter short with me. His remarks evidently had great weight with the council, and exerted a soothing effect on all of them. At this point I thought it a meet season to impress upon their minds that I was of some consequence in the world, and asked leave to speak for myself, which was granted. Thereupon I launched forth in an oration, the chief acting as interpreter, and retailing it to the circle sentence by sentence:

"Buenos Senores! Me mucho Grande Americano capitan, mismo commodant mucho mass, mucha barca, mucha galeta, muchos soldados, muchos marinarios. Me tene mucho mucho big guns, bastante poquito mismo bastante, cutlass, pistols mucho bastante. Vuestros hombres buenos per me, mi marinarios, mi soldados, buenos per vos. Othro corso usted malo rumpe me," &c. &c. &c. In such a jumble of Spanish, English and Indian, duly set off with grimace and gesture, I gave them to understand that they were dealing with no inferior personage, but with one who was at home as good as the president; one having at command abundance of steamships and sailing vessels of all sorts, with soldiers and mariners, big guns and little guns, pistols and cutlasses. That if they were good to me they would receive good from me and mine; but that, if they did me any harm, men would come from North America in numbers as incalculable as the hairs of their heads, and kill every mother's son of them. Furthermore, if they would take me to some white settlement, whether American, English, French or Spanish, I would order the white people to give them rum, tobacco, flour, rice, sugar and tea. Of course the white men could do no less than obey, and they would thus be enabled to indulge themselves in luxuries almost without limit.

It was evident, at a glance, that my speech was seasonable, and took effect in the right quarter. Their eyes stood out with wonder, and the sternness of their countenances was relaxed. They acquiesced in the proposal to postpone final action for the present, and see what could be made out of me before doing their worst. In a few days, they said, they would take me to "Holland;" but, no matter what time was limited, that "undiscovered country" seemed continually further off,—"a name" without any "local habitation." Their conduct in this was determined, as I was afterwards assured, by the fact that they were entirely undecided what to do with me. They longed for the good things I had told them of, and their greedy appetites could only be satisfied by taking me to a white settlement. On the other hand, they were painfully suspicious that I meant to give them the slip, and dreaded the result of bringing me into the vicinity of any settlement; while, at the same time, my grandiloquent assumptions and lofty threats made them shrink from the thought of doing me serious harm. The big guns and little guns greatly disturbed their imaginations. In short, I seemed to them an ugly customer—bad to keep, and bad to get rid of. They temporized, therefore, promised and hesitated, and postponed, and promised again. There was no use in trying to hurry their movements. So I gave them line upon line, seeking every opportunity to deepen the troublesome impression that they assumed a mighty responsibility when they made me a prisoner, and that their welfare depended greatly on the issue.

CHAPTER IV

Corey Inlet—Another disappointment—A hunting frolic with an unpleasant termination—Moving of the camp—Aimless wanderings—Alarm—A marriage treaty and an unsuccessful suitor—Laws of marriage—Qualifications of a husband—Feminine quarrels—A marriage in high life—Dressing meat—Profaneness—Absence of religious ideas—Mysterious ceremony—Reasons for abstaining from religious instruction—The metals—State of the arts in Patagonia—Tailoring—Fashion.

The next move of the tribe brought us within about a mile of Corey Inlet. The day after we halted, in full view of the south Atlantic, on looking out upon the water, two masts were plainly descried, evidently those of some vessel running down to this inlet. On going up an elevation commanding a better view, it proved to be a topsail schooner. She had undoubtedly mistaken this false cape for Cape Virgin, at the entrance of the Straits of Magellan. I pointed out the vessel to the Indians, and requested them to take me to the shore, that I might, if possible, communicate with her and be ransomed. After some delay, they complied; but, as we approached the beach, she was seen suddenly to haul off the shore and stand down the coast, having probably found out her mistake. We made all possible haste to gain the beach before she could have time to pass out of sight. I mounted a tall cliff, where I could distinctly see the men on deck, and, standing on the horse's back, waved my jacket, and made every possible demonstration to attract their notice. All in vain. The little vessel sailed steadily on, as if in mockery of my hopes. I watched her receding figure with an aching heart, till she vanished from sight. Thoughts of home and its familiar circle, of lost enjoyments, and of the suffering that must be a guest there, had long tantalized my sleeping and embittered my waking dreams. These were quickened and concentrated in a burning focus, by the light of such a vision from the world of my past existence, only to inflict the keener torture upon my sensibilities. My situation became more intolerable by every fresh disappointment. It was almost enough to drive me mad. Must I, then, give up all hope of rescue?

A few minutes passed, and the tempest of feeling passed with them. Reflection convinced me that the indulgence of such feelings was not only useless, but actually pernicious, as tending to unfit me for rational and successful contrivance. My condition, truly, was dreadful; so much the more necessary was it to exercise the most calm and patient and self-possessed prudence, in order to devise and execute any purpose of escape. Like the surgeon who looks with steady nerve on the quivering frame subjected to his knife, I must nerve myself to look the gloomy problem of my lot, without shrinking, fully in the face, and keep my emotions, in all circumstances, strictly under the control of the calculating judgment; a maxim, like many others, much easier uttered now than to be thought of then, and far easier asserted than exemplified. Fully bent on effecting my deliverance in some way, to the discovery of which all possible ingenuity was to be directed, my resolutions of self-control were heroic enough. But to fulfil them,—to repress and disregard all those sympathies to which my whole being was bound,—this was indeed labor, too great, I often feared, to be accomplished. When the stress of inward conflict oppressed me, I would spring from my crouching-place in the lodge, rush into the open air, and seize upon every object that could in any degree divert attention and divide my thoughts. These exertions, with God's blessing, sufficed to restore, in some tolerable measure, the mental equilibrium, and to rescue me from the dominion of feelings the unrestrained action of which would have driven me to madness.

During our stay of three or four days at this encampment, I had become so wearied with the monotony of their idleness, broken only by their desperate gambling,—the only thing, besides the chase, with which the Indians occupied themselves,—that for variety's sake, to divert my often-desponding moods, and to kill time, which hung heavily on my hands, I concluded to go out on a hunting frolic. Having procured a horse of the chief, and encased my lower extremities in a pair of native boots, much warmer than the ship shoes in which I had endured the cold, I set out with quite a party. We had gone six or eight miles, when I stopped for a short time, the rest of the troop riding off without regarding me. On remounting my charger, I put him to his utmost speed, in order to overtake them. While driving on at a furious rate, he stumbled and came to the ground, throwing his luckless rider over his head twenty feet or more, upon the hard, frozen ground. One ankle was severely sprained, and my whole body more or less bruised. So severe, indeed, was the shock, that I have occasional reminders of it to this day. No time was to be lost; and, with considerable effort, and no little pain, I succeeded in remounting. The swelling of my foot soon made my borrowed boots extremely uncomfortable, and I wished myself safely back at the lodge; but, at whatever expense of suffering, I had no resource but to follow the hunters till such time as they should see fit to return. The remembrance of that day's torment will not soon be lost. We arrived at the camp late in the evening; and, having been unsuccessful in the chase, went supperless to bed. On crawling into the hut and removing my boots, a sad sight was disclosed; but there was no present remedy. Dragging myself wearily into my corner, I had just crouched upon the skin, which had served for a saddle during the day and was still reeking from the horse's back, when a great dog came along, and threw his whole weight upon the lame foot, causing me to scream aloud for the pain. I drew back the serviceable foot, and gave him a kick that sent him through the fire and against the front of the lodge. Sleep kept at a distance till near morning, when I gained a brief oblivion of suffering.

Day at last dawned, and with the morning's light came the busy note of preparation for removal. Down came the tents; the squaws packing up the furniture, and the Indians chasing and lassoing their horses. The noise and confusion, disagreeable enough under any circumstances, made the scene no inapt representative of chaos, from which I was glad to be delivered on the most expeditious terms possible; and I was easily persuaded to try my fortune again in the chase, more especially as we had nothing for breakfast. No words can do more than partial justice to one of these moving scenes. Not only the skin roofs of their wigwams, but the stakes and poles which constitute the frames, are carried along with them. Their furniture gives them little trouble, seldom consisting of more than the skins on which they sleep, an ox-horn tinder-box, a few sticks for roasting meat, and a leathern water-bucket. Tents and furniture are all packed together on their horses' backs. The pappooses in travelling are lashed to a kind of wooden sledge, rounded at the ends like sleigh-runners, and crossed with narrow slats, that bind the parts strongly together. The little brats are bound upon these machines, which are so shaped that their heads and feet are much below the general level of their bodies,—a very uncomfortable position for the youngsters, if they have as much sensibility to pain as other children, of which I incline to doubt, as they are inured from birth to almost every species of hardship. The sledge, with its living burden, is thrown across the horse's back, and made fast to the load. The mother mounts to the top of the pack, resting her feet on the horse's neck, and armed with a cudgel, with which she vigorously belabors the beast, right and left. The pappooses, not liking the quarters assigned to them, set up a general squalling. Mothers and maiden aunts join in full chorus, drawling out, at the top of their voices, "Hōrī! mutty, mutty! Hōrī! mutty, mutty!" without the least change, to the thousandth repetition. All these arrangements are made with remarkable celerity—in thirty minutes not a tent is left standing, but the whole tribe, their tenements and chattels, wives and brats, are all packed upon horses, and the motley cavalcade moves off like an army of beggars on horseback.

BREAKING UP OF CAMP

On the present occasion the movement was delayed, while we rode in search of something to eat. The chase was unsuccessful, scarcely enough being obtained to more than sharpen our appetites for dinner. The scanty meal being over, the whole company began their journey, which in its tortuous windings was not unlike that of the Israelites in the wilderness, but unlike that in the respect that we seemed to have no particular destination or object, except to explore new hunting-grounds, and gratify the capricious restlessness of the Indians. One very desirable end was answered,—we got enough to eat, as we were successful in killing a large quantity of game. The Indians, it was noticeable, were never at a loss to find their camps. So familiar did they seem with all their haunts and the general shape of the country, that though the surface presented to my eye scarcely any distinguishable way-marks, they would strike off from any point, however distant, and go with unerring aim straight to their tents. In returning laden with booty to our new homes, I was surprised to observe no indications whatever of water in the vicinity; a singular departure, at first sight, from their invariable custom, so far as I had noticed. Very soon the squaws issued from their huts, each with her leathern bucket. Curiosity prompted me to follow them a little way, when a spring was discovered, from which they had to dip the water with their ox-horn cups till the buckets were filled.

About this time a new phase of life presented itself, to cast light on an important item of the social economy established in Patagonia. Looking out of our wigwam one evening just at dusk, I noticed an unusual concourse of Indians about two hundred yards distant. There were fifty or more, headed by one of the most ruffianly rascals in the tribe, marching in the direction of our lodge. I spoke to the chief about it, whereupon he went immediately to the back of the hut, and sat down on his little bed, his cutlass hanging beside him from a knot of one of the stakes. This he took down, laid it across his knees, and folded his arms. Something, I saw, was wrong. In anticipation of the worst that might befall me, I had found, a short time before, the handle of an old knife among the chief's trumpery, and also an odd blade; these I had put together, and the chief permitted me to carry it about my person, the only weapon he allowed me. I now planted myself on my knees beside him, and prepared to sell my life as dearly as possible, should the mob enter with evil designs towards me. The consciousness that I was in their power, and was sure to have the worst of any serious quarrel, made it my study to keep the peace with them as far as circumstances would admit; but there was a limit to my control of events, a very narrow limit, which I had constant reason to fear would be overborne by the impetuous hatred of my enemies, when nothing would be left but desperate resistance. Such a crisis seemed near, when the chief was himself reduced to a defensive attitude, and was indeed besieged in his own lodge.

The motley throng surrounded the hut, their numbers constantly swelled by fresh arrivals; some were squat upon the ground, others peeping through the crevices. Presently one of the number addressed the chief, and the two conversed for some time in a low and unintelligible, but decided and emphatic tone. The crowd outside appeared to be a good deal excited, and kept up a continuous hum of rapid conversation. I looked and listened, with mingled curiosity and dread, while the chief repeated the same thing over and over again, in a firm, authoritative tone, tinged with anger. Unable to conjecture what was on foot, or to bear any longer the agony of suspense, I patted him familiarly on his naked breast, told him he had "a good heart," begged that he would not suffer the Indians to harm me. "You go sleep," was his answer; "no Indians come into this house to-night." I inquired what they were after, but no answer was vouchsafed, and he resumed his mysterious colloquy with the outsiders. The idea of sleeping under such circumstances was out of the question; I was wide awake, and bent on keeping so,—sorely bewildered at the strange goings on, and not a little terrified, but holding fast by my sole weapon of defence, and waiting a favorable opportunity to interpose another inquiry. The chief turned his head; and, perceiving my vigilance, repeated in an angry tone his injunction to sleep. This was a drop too much; and, clasping my arms about his dirty neck, patting his breast, and looking (with as confiding an air as I could assume) into his dull eyes, I begged him to speak to me, to tell me what these men wanted. "Do they want to break my head?"

"The men don't want to hurt you," he said; "Indian wants a girl for his wife; poor Indian, very poor, got no horses nor anything else. I won't give him the woman."

So speedy a descent from the height of my fears was not satisfactory; it was impossible to credit this explanation of such a formidable scene. I apprehended that it was a pure fiction, extemporized for the purpose of quieting me; but, as he seemed more communicative, I swallowed my doubts, and questioned him further. "What does poor Indian say?"

"Says he'll steal plenty horses when we get where they are, and give the woman plenty of grease. Says he is a good hunter, good thief."

These high titles to consideration did not seem to be admitted by the party they were offered to conciliate; on the contrary, the chief pronounced him a sleepy mink-skin of a fellow,—no thief at all; one that would never own a horse in the world. This opinion, which he was good enough to favor me with, he communicated to the party chiefly concerned, telling him that he was a poor, good-for-nothing Indian, he should not have the woman, and that was the end of it. After a little more jabber, and abundance of wrangling, the mob dispersed, much to my relief. Satisfied, by further conversation on the subject with old Parosilver, whose triumph over the mutiny had put him into better temper than usual, that the affair did not imminently concern my safety or welfare, I lay down to rest.

In answer to further inquiries,—for I must plead guilty to a good deal of curiosity in respect of the poor Indian and his blasted hopes,—I was informed that without the chief's consent no marriage was permitted; that, in his judgment, no Indian who was not an accomplished rogue,—particularly in the horse-stealing line,—an expert hunter, able to provide plenty of meat and grease, was fit to have a wife on any terms. He never gave his consent for such lazy ones to take an extra rib; but, he very considerately added, all the difference it made was that some one else had to support the squaw till her suitor proved himself worthy, and acquired sufficient wealth to justify taking her to his wigwam; and, if he cared much for his coury, he would not be long in earning her; it would make him a first-rate thief,— the most indispensable title to favor in the tribe. It appeared that the possession of two horses, one for himself and one for his intended, was regarded as the proper outfit in a matrimonial adventure.

The women are somewhat given to quarrelling among themselves; and, when their "combativeness" is once active, they fight like tigers. Jealousy is a frequent occasion. If a squaw suspects her liege lord of undue familiarity with a rival, she darts upon the fair enchantress with the fury of a wild beast; then ensues such a pounding, scratching and hair-pulling, as beggars description. The gay deceiver, if taken by surprise, slips quietly out, and stands at a safe distance to watch the progress of the combat, generally chuckling at the fun with great complacency. A crowd gathers round to cheer on the rivals; and the rickety wigwam, under the effect of the squall within, creaks and shivers like a ship in the wind's eye.

While the contract of marriage is so jealously regarded by the chief as to be subject to a veto in every case where a proposed match appears in his eyes unsuitable, the ceremony is literally nothing at all. Due sanction having been given by the supreme authority, the bridegroom takes home his bride for better or worse, without any of the festivity which graces similar occasions elsewhere. About this time,—for, as I had no means of journalizing my experience, or even keeping the reckoning of weeks and months, it is quite impossible to assign dates,—a matrimonial transaction took place, accompanied by unusual solemnities. The rank of one party, and the extraordinary accessories of the occasion, will justify a particular notice of this "marriage in high life."

One evening, the chief, his four wives, two daughters, an infant granddaughter, and myself, were scattered about the lodge, enveloped in a smoke of unusual strength and density. While the others sat around as unconcerned as so many pieces of bacon, I lay flat, with my face close to the ground, and my head covered with a piece of guanaco-skin, the only position in which it was possible to gain any relief from the stifling fumigation. While in this attitude, I fancied I heard the tramp of many feet without, and a confused muttering, as if a multitude of Indians were talking together. Presently a hoarse voice sounded in front, evidently aimed at the ears of some one within, to which the chief promptly replied. I caught a few words,—enough to satisfy me that I was not the subject of their colloquy, but that there was a lady in the case,—and listened curiously, without any of the fright which grew out of the previous negotiations. The conversation grew animated, and the equanimity of his high mightiness the chief was somewhat disturbed. I cast a penetrating glance into the smoke at the female members of our household, to discern, if possible; whether any one of them was specially interested. One look was sufficient; the chief's daughter (who, by the way, was a quasi widow, with one hopeful scion springing up by her side) sat listening to the conversation, with anxiety and apprehension visible in every feature. Her mother sat near her, her chin resting upon her hand, with an anxious and thoughtful expression of countenance. The invisible speaker without, it soon appeared, was an unsuccessful suitor of the daughter, and had come with his friends to press his claim. He urged his suit, if not with classic, with "earnest" eloquence, but with success ill proportioned to his efforts. The chief told him he was a poor, good-for-nothing fellow, had no horses, and was unfit to be his son-in-law, or any one else's. The outsider was not to be so easily put off; he pressed his suit with fresh energy, affirming that his deficiency of horses was from want of opportunity, not from lack of will or ability to appropriate the first that came within his reach. On the contrary, he claimed to be as ingenious and accomplished a thief as ever swung a lasso or ran off a horse, and a mighty hunter besides, whose wife would never suffer for want of grease. The inexorable chief hereat got considerably excited, told him he was a poor devil, and might be off with himself; he wouldn't talk any more about it.

The suppliant, as a last resort, appealed to the fair one herself, begging her to smile on his suit, and assuring her, with marked emphasis, that, if successful in his aspirations, he would give her plenty of grease. At this last argument she was unable to resist longer, but entreated her father to sanction their union. But the hard-hearted parent, not at all mollified by this appeal from his decision to an inferior tribunal, broke out in a towering passion, and poured forth a torrent of abuse. The mother here interposed, and besought him not to be angry with the young folks, but to deal more gently and considerately with them. She even hinted that he might have done injustice to the young man. He might turn out a smarter man than he had credit for. He might—who knew?—make a fine chief yet, possess plenty of horses, and prove a highly eligible match for their daughter. The old fellow had been (for him) quite moderate, but this was too much. His rage completely mastered him. He rose up, seized the pappoose's cradle, and hurled it violently out of doors, and the other chattels appertaining to his daughter went after it in rapid succession. He then ordered her to follow her goods instanter, with which benediction she departed, responding with a smile of satisfaction, doubtless anticipating the promised luxuries of her new home, the vision of which, through the present tempest, fortified her mind against its worst perils. Leaving the lodge, she gathered up her scattered effects, and, accompanied by her mother, the bridal party disappeared.

The chief sat on his horse-skin couch, his legs crossed partly under him, looking sour enough. Presently the bride and her mother returned, and now began the second scene. The chief no sooner recognized them than a sound—something between a grunt and a growl, but much nearer the latter than the former, and in a decided crescendo—gave warning of a fresh eruption. The rumbling grew more emphatic, and suddenly his fury burst on the head of his wife. Seizing her by the hair, he hurled her violently to the ground, and beat her with his clenched fists till I thought he would break every bone in her body, and reduce her substance to a jelly. Perhaps I was a little hard-hearted, but she had been one of my bitterest enemies, and I had a feeling that if some of her ill-will to me could be beaten out of her, I could be easily resigned to her fate. The drubbing ended, she rose and muttered something he did not like. He replied by a violent blow on the side of her head, that sent her staggering to the further end of the hut. This last argument was decisive, and she kept her huge mouth closed for the night. There was a silent pause for some minutes, and, without another word, we ranged ourselves for repose. I thought the old heathen's conscience troubled him through the night; his sleep was broken, and he appeared very restless. Early the next morning he went to the lodge of the newly-married pair, and had a long chat with them. They thought him rather severe upon them at first; but, after a good deal of diplomacy, a better understanding was brought about. The young people could hardly get over a sense of the indignities they had received; but in the course of the day they returned, bag and baggage, to the old chief's tent, and made it their permanent abode.

We now moved in a westerly direction, and on the way succeeded in capturing a good deal of game. Their mode of dealing with the carcass of the guanaco is enough to dissipate whatever appetizing qualities the meat—in itself very palatable—would otherwise possess. It was no uncommon circumstance, while the squaws were removing the hide, to see the dogs tugging at the other extremity, the women, meantime, crying out "Eh! Ah!" in a dissuasive, though not angry, tone. If the animals become too audacious, the ire of their mistresses is kindled, and they break out with "Cashuran cashahy!" a phrase equivalent to that which, in English, directs its object to a region unmentionable in ears polite.

The Indians have, strictly speaking, no profane expressions. I never could learn that they worshipped or had any idea of a Supreme Being. The only observance which bore any aspect of religion was associated with something we should little think of as an object of adoration—the tobacco-pipe;—though, how far this is, in fact, an object of idolatry in Christian lands, it might not become me to speculate. The only occasions on which the Indians discovered any appearance of devotion were those of smoking. This may have been only a symptom of intoxication, but the reader may judge for himself.

A group of a dozen or more assemble,—sometimes in a wigwam, sometimes in the open air. A vessel made of a piece of hide bent into a saucer-shape while green and afterwards hardened, or sometimes an ox-horn, filled with water, is set on the ground. A stone pipe is filled with the scrapings of a wood resembling yellow ebony, mixed with finely-cut tobacco. The company then lay themselves in a circle flat on their faces, their mantles drawn up to the tops of their heads. The pipe is lighted. One takes it into his mouth and inhales as much smoke as he can swallow; the others take it in succession, till all have become satisfied. By the time the second smoker is fully charged, the first begins a series of groanings and gruntings, with a slight trembling of the head, the smoke slowly oozing out at the nostrils. The groaning soon becomes general, and waxes louder, till it swells into a hideous howling, enough to frighten man or beast. The noise gradually dies away. They remain a short time in profound silence, and each imbibes a draught of water. Then succeeds another interval of silence, observed with the most profound and devotional gravity. At length arise, and slowly disperse. Now, this may or may not have been a form of worship; but the circumstances attending it, the numbers uniformly engaged in it the formality with which it was invariably conducted, the solemnity of visage, the reverential grimace, the prostration, the silence, the trembling,—these, and traits of expression which are more easily discerned and remembered than described, gave me a decided impression that the whole had a superstitious meaning. The natural operation of the tobacco, and of the substance mixed with it, might explain part of the symptoms,—the writhing and groaning,—but these appeared to be a good deal in excess, and there were other features of the case which appeared to require another solution.

I never asked any explanation. The mystery which savage tribes are so apt to throw around their religious rites, and their resentment at any unhallowed curiosity, I was not inclined to meddle with or provoke. If my conjectures were just as to the nature of this ceremony, inquiry might lead to unpleasant consequences. Ignorance appeared, on the whole, safer than knowledge of good or evil, gained at the risk of being caught trespassing on things forbidden. If any one thinks my precaution excessive, he is at liberty to take a different course whenever he finds himself in the jurisdiction of Parosilver, or any other Patagonian chief.

The inquiry may arise, especially in the mind of the religious reader, whether I attempted to impart to my captors any knowledge of God, his attributes and laws. The answer is quite ready,—No, and for a variety of reasons. The writer did not understand enough of either Spanish or Indian to communicate intelligible ideas on any matters beyond the range of the senses, and Patagonia is pretty barren of sensible phenomena, which made my stock of words more limited than it might have been under more favorable circumstances. There was no finding "tongues in trees," or "books in the running brooks;" the land possesses neither in numbers sufficient to be conversable. "Sermons in stones," even, must have been of very pebbly dimensions, and of no great weight. Had this difficulty been removed, I confess I had no great desire to surmount it. I was the object of suspicion and hostility. My life was in constant danger. To diminish, as far as possible, the causes of dislike, to mitigate their ferocious hate, to elude occasions of mischief, to delay what I feared could not be very long prevented, was my continual study. If the reader is not satisfied with this account of my conduct, I am sorry for it, but cannot afford any words of contrition. It is vastly easier, I may hint to the objector, to prescribe another's duties than to judge of one's own, especially where the two parties are in circumstances so widely differing. The Patagonians need the gospel—and the law—as much as any people I could name from personal observation. There was no trace of instruction imparted at a previous period, and the reception Christianity would meet with among them is yet to be discovered.

Their pipes are made of a hard red stone, the bowl dug out with whatever iron or steel implement is at command to the dimensions of an ordinary clay pipe, the stem about an inch square, and three inches long, with a small perforation. A copper or brass tube, about two inches long, is fitted to the stem, and serves as a mouth-piece. This is made by bending or hammering a metallic plate about a small round stick, and soldering or cementing it with a glutinous substance thickened with earth.

The copper, brass and iron, seen among them, was probably procured from unfortunate vessels wrecked on their coast. I was informed by Captain Morton, of whom the persevering reader will know more hereafter, that he had touched at Sea Bear Bay for a harbor, and saw there great quantities of iron pumps, ships' hanging knees, and other gear, from wrecks of vessels of all sizes. As he was bound for the land of gold, he thought it scarcely worth his while to collect the baser metals. Had he been homeward bound, he might have obtained a valuable cargo.

As ornaments, bits of brass and copper, of silver and German silver, have a high value among the Indians, and when the metals are plenty such adornment is very common. The children's shoes have small oval pieces sewed on in front, and they appear on other parts of their dress. When scarce, they are more seldom seen. Blacksmithing in Patagonia is something of the rudest. Two hard flat stones do duty, the one as anvil, and the other as hammer. Of the effect of heat in making the metals malleable, and of the art of tempering, the people have no knowledge. To make a knife, they take a piece of iron hoop, or iron in any practicable shape, and hammer away upon it at a provokingly slow rate. Their blows are not heavy enough to do much execution; but they keep up a constant tap, tap, tap, hour by hour, till the iron is flattened to the required shape and dimensions. It is then rubbed on a smooth stone till it is worn down to an edge, and finally inserted into a wooden handle. Sometimes melted lead is poured into the handle, but lead appeared to be a scarce commodity. All mechanic arts, if they deserve the name, are in an equally rude and primitive stage. The simplicity of these people's ideas is indeed extraordinary. In invention or constructiveness they are babes. A Yankee boy, six years old, would be a prodigy among them,—a miracle of genius.

An opportunity was afforded, while in camp, to see some specimens of their tailoring or mantua-making achievements;—either term is appropriate, as the male and female dress do not differ in form, and but slightly in the mode of adjustment. The mantle or blanket is worn around the shoulders; those of the women are fastened together by the corners under the chin with a stick for a pin; the men hold theirs around them with their hands, except that when hunting they tie a string around the waist.

The skins of young guanacos are selected for mantles, on account of the superior fineness and softness of the hair. Nearly a dozen skins are used for a single mantle, as a large part of each is esteemed unfit for use, and thrown away. The skins, while green, are stretched to their utmost tension on the ground to dry. When partially dried, they are scraped on the inside with a stone sharpened like a gun-flint, sprinkled the while with water, to facilitate the operation. When the surface is made tolerably smooth, and of a pretty uniform thickness, it is actively scoured with a coarse-grained stone, till it has a bright polish. The skin is again dried, then crumpled and twisted in the hands till it becomes perfectly soft and pliable. The thread, as has been stated, is made from the sinews of the ostrich. These are extracted by the exertion of great strength, and divided into strings about the size of ordinary shoe-thread. They are then twisted, the ends are scraped to a point, and when dry become stiff; they are now ready for use.

Two pieces of skin are cut to fit each other. The tailoress (for all the work, from the curing of the skins to the last results, is done by the squaws) holds the edges together with the left hand, and drills them for sewing with a sharpened nail, held between the first two fingers of the right hand; the pointed thread, held between the finger and thumb, is inserted and drawn through, and so the work goes on. The stitches are tolerably fine, and a very neat seam is made. Other pieces are added, and when the whole is finished the seams are rubbed smooth with a bone. The fur being worn inside, there remains the work of outside decoration. With a due quantity of clay, blood, charcoal and grease, amalgamated for the purpose, the artist arms herself with a stick for a brush, and executes divers figures in black, on a red ground; which, if intended to shadow forth men, require a vigorous imagination to detect the purpose. They might pass for unhappy ghosts (if a little more ethereal in composition), or for deformed trees. They bear a rude resemblance to a chair in profile, or a figure 4; and are thickly disposed over the whole surface, in the attitude sometimes vulgarly termed "spoon-fashion." The garment is now complete; the edges are carefully trimmed with a knife, and the fabric is thrown over the shoulders, with the infallible certainty of fitting as closely as the native tastes require. There is no trial of patience in smoothing obstinate wrinkles. A "genteel fit" is the easiest thing in the world; wherein Patagonian tailors have decidedly the advantage of their fellow-craftsmen in civilized lands.

CHAPTER V

Inclement weather—State of my wardrobe—Attempts to deprive me of my clothes—Powwow and horse-killing—Hair-combing extraordinary—Remedy for rheumatism—Sickness—Turn barber—A cold bath—Fasting—Discovery of my watch, and its effect—I am made showman—Lion-hunt—Successful chase.

At our next halt we encamped in a deep, swampy valley. The weather was cold and stormy; rain, snow, sleet and hail, fell alternately, but did not accumulate on the earth to any considerable depth. Fitful gusts of wind came sweeping through the camp, making the wigwams shake fearfully. Our old lodge gallantly rode out the gale; but, either owing to its straining and working in the storm, or to some defects in the original structure, leaked shockingly all night. I was repeatedly awakened by a stream of cold water running under me. Giving the skin roof a few knocks to lighten it of its watery burden, and shaking the wet skin which constituted my couch, I would throw myself down, and resign myself to repose; but before quiet was fairly restored, another inundation would drive me to my feet. The night wore away with me, wet, cold and sleepless. After daybreak I rose, and continued for two hours in vigorous exercise to restore warmth to my chilled frame, before the Indians were astir. Fires were then kindled, and matters began to assume a more cheerful appearance.

The weather, quite cool on my first landing, had grown gradually colder, and was becoming inclement. I was scantily prepared to endure the severity of winter. My under-garments, as before related, were desperately expended in trying to signal passing vessels. Cravat and pocket-handkerchief were appropriated to the adornment of the women in our household, to the no small envy of less favored ones. My sole article of linen was in shreds, and of a color that would afford matter for speculation to a jury of washerwomen. Stockings and shoes were sadly dilapidated; coat and trousers were glazed with dirt and grease till they shone like a glass bottle. The contents of my pockets were all confiscated,— purse, keys, knife, &c.,—and a pair of pistols, of the use of which my captors knew nothing, were taken to pieces, and the brass mountings suspended about the necks of the chief's wives. In short, my outer man was nigh unto perishing, and I had no visible resources to arrest or repair the process of time, while I was not sufficiently inured to the climate to adopt the native dress without serious risk to health. But none of these things were allowed to trouble me. I took no thought for the morrow, but, according to the scriptural injunction, suffered the morrow to take care for the things of itself, esteeming sufficient unto each day the evil thereof.

At an early period of my captivity, the chief and some other Indians had cast a longing eye on my clothes, and tried to seduce me into parting with them. They offered no compulsion in the matter, but resorted to all manner of tricks. It seemed that they thought a white man could afford to go without dressing. I explained to them that, having always worn clothes,—having in infancy, even, unlike Patagonian piccaninnies, been externally protected against the fresh air,—it was quite impossible for me to change my habits without the hazard of my life; and, if I should die in consequence of yielding to their wishes, they were reminded they would lose the valuable ransom they expected for me. This reasoning proved convincing; greatly as they longed for my wardrobe, they more desired rum and tobacco, and I was permitted the undisturbed enjoyment of the scanty covering left me.

The storm continued for two days and nights; on the third day it cleared up. About mid-day, observing a crowd of Indians together with a huge jargon of tongues, I learned, on inquiry, that a horse was to be killed; a matter which, it appeared, was always the occasion of a solemn powwow. On reaching the spot, a poor old beast, lean and lank, with a lariat about his neck, stood surrounded by some fifty Indians. The squaws were singing, in stentorian tones, "Ye! Ye! Yup! Yup! Lar, lapuly, yapuly!" with a repetition that became unendurable, and drove me to a respectful distance. The horse's fore-legs were fast bound together, a violent push forward threw him heavily to the ground, and he was speedily despatched with a knife; anticipating, by a few days, the ordinary course of nature. Soon after my return to the wigwam, a huge portion of the carcass was sent to our quarters and hung up, to furnish our next meals! After being duly dressed by the women, with the aid of the dogs, and scorched and smoked according to usage, it was served up,—my only alternative to starvation. Famine has no scruples of delicacy; if the reader is disgusted, he is in a state of sympathy with the writer.

Early the next day we (literally) pulled up stakes, and were on the move; and, after journeying all day, encamped in a situation very like the one we left in the morning. The Indians spent their time, as usual, in gambling and in combing each other's hair, with a brush made of stiff dry roots, tied up together. The operator received as a fee the game captured in the process. The reader will excuse a more explicit statement of what, though less abominable than cannibalism, is hardly less repulsive.

One evening our family circle were seated round a fire, which sent up volumes of smoke sufficiently dense to suit a savage of the most exacting taste, and which drove me, as usual, to the back part of the hut, where I lay flat on my face. One of the chief's wives was inveighing against me, as was her wont, and a second occasionally joined in the strain, by way of chorus. A third was cracking the bones of a guanaco, that her son Cohanaco might eat the marrow. The fourth and last of the women was attending to a piece of meat for our supper, fixed on a forked stick, in the smoke. Two sons were engaged, as usual, in doing nothing, except occasionally begging a little of the marrow, and scraping their dirty legs with a sheath-knife, by way of diversion; sundry by-plays, and little pieces of mischief, served to fill up the spare minutes. The old chief, who had been silently regarding the scene, now commenced talking, in a low, mumbling, guttural tone, to one of his wives. She was busily eying the toasting-fork, and studying the process of cooking; but, at her husband's instance, left them, and drew from their repository of tools a sharpened nail fixed in a wooden handle, like an awl. The chief stretched himself on the ground, face downwards; a surgical operation was plainly impending. What could the matter be? Had the chief, in the excess of his plumpness, burst open, like ripe fruit, requiring to be sewed up? I drew my head from beneath the protection I had provided against the smoke, and rose on my knees, to get a better view; the huge, black, greasy monster lay extended at his full length, his wife pinched up the skin on his back, pierced it with her awl, and continued the process till a number of perforations were made, from which the blood oozed slowly. I asked the meaning of this operation, and was told by the chief that he had pains in his back, for which this was the best remedy. Blood-letting, it seemed, is no monopoly of the faculty. I told him that in my country we applied, in such cases, a liquid called opodeldoc, an infallible remedy, and promised to procure him some when we got to Holland. This was henceforth added to my list of inducements.

The old fellow righted himself, and leaned against one of the pillars of his palace; one of his partners pulled up the toasting-fork, and jerked the half-roasted and more than sufficiently smoked meat upon the ground, seized the knife which the boys had been playing with, and cut the mess into liberal pieces, which were thrown broadcast on either side. The chief's appetite did not appear to be affected either by his indisposition or by the extraordinary remedy applied; his portion of the cárne disappeared behind his great white teeth with a haste that seemed to involve no waste.

Rheumatic affections, they told me, are very common among them; the chief showed me the arm of one of his wives, which was scarred from the wrist to the shoulder by the awl; and the operation was afterwards performed on other members of the family.

Again we took up the line of march, travelling, as near as I could judge, west-north-west, and killing a quantity of game, both guanaco and ostrich. But the hardship of my life, aggravated by a constant flesh diet, and that eaten half raw, and at irregular seasons,—often going two days without food,—had, by this time, brought on a dysentery. This was no more than I had expected; but I knew of no remedy, and had to endure it as I could. We encamped, on the second day, near the banks of the river Gallegos; a fine spring of water issued from the river-bank into a low marshy ground, skirting the margin of the stream. By this time my illness had increased, till I felt unfit to travel further, and began to think that death could not be distant. No change of diet was practicable, and there was nothing to counteract its effect on my system. The pain and weariness of travelling did their part to aggravate the disorder; and mental discouragement—the sickness of hope deferred—completed my prostration. No human being in that desolate land cared for my sufferings, more than they would for those of a dog. Worn out with the constant irritations of a state of existence odious to every sensibility, tired and disheartened, but for one thought I could have gladly laid myself down to die, to get at once and forever beyond the reach of my savage tormentors. The thought of home, of wife and child, of friends and country, and all the unutterable emotions that respond to these precious names, at once tortured and strengthened me. These, and the thought that perhaps, after patient endurance, Divine Providence would restore me to the objects of my famished affections, made life still dear. These strengthened me to suffer and to strive.

As I crawled out of the lodge, to look upon the sun, and breathe the pure air, and be refreshed by breezes untainted with the breath of cruel men, it came into my mind that some palatable or even tolerable species of plant or root would be wholesome for me. On looking about, there presented itself a specimen of large dock, such as is common in the United States; a weed of humble pretensions, but why not worthy of a trial? With what strength remained at command, I began a process of "extracting roots," with good success. Taking a quantity into the hut, and roasting them in hot ashes, they were found to be not distasteful; I filled my pockets with them, and abandoned flesh-diet for a little time, to the sensible, though gradual, relief of my sufferings. Fortunately we had a season of bad weather, which prevented any advance movement for four or five days, and gave me time partially to recover strength. I could not sooner have kept my seat on a horse; and, if the alternative had been presented, the Indians, as I very well knew, would sooner have knocked me on the head than have allowed me to hinder their march for a day. A powwow was held over another horse, unserviceable alive, and therefore marked for diet; but this time I did not compete for any part of his carcass, my pocket-stores being quite sufficient, and more attractive. But in the fate of the poor beast I read a warning to myself, to make haste and get well enough to move at the first signal.

Away again,—this time facing about, and passing down the river. I needed rest; but, at whatever expense of suffering, needs must when a certain old gentleman drives. At the next stopping-place my services were called into requisition in a new department. One forenoon, as I sauntered towards our wigwam, after a stroll among the smutty huts, to kill time and divert painful thoughts, I was hailed from within by the chief, "Arke, Boney!" On entering, he appeared to be conversing, in low, gurgling sounds, with his lately-married daughter, who was running her hands through the shaggy hair of her young hope, as she talked. Something was plainly wrong in the youngster's top-knot, and some unpleasant task in relation thereto was as plainly about to be imposed upon me. The chief resolved my doubts, by ordering me to cut off a portion of the shag; I objected a want of the proper implements, but the mother silenced me by producing an old pair of scissors, in no condition to cut anything. Calling for a file, the rusty edges were brought into a tolerable state, and I approached the task. Such a sight! If the hair now would have obeyed a mesmeric pass, without the need of manual contact,—if the job could be performed with closed eyes, and insensible nostrils, and absent mind! Faugh! I hurried through the penance, hiding disgust, and assuming the appearance of good will, and made good my escape into the fresh air. And so I must turn barber, and, in all likelihood, have the dirty heads of half the tribe put under my nose! What would come next?

Our next move took us across the river Gallegos, in shoal water, barely up to the horses' knees. The current was rapid, and masses of floating ice were swept along with it. When half way across, my horse took fright, reared, and, in attempting a sudden turn, precipitated me into the water, and fell heavily upon me. The ducking and the bruise together were severe, and, among other disasters, the crystal of my watch was broken by the shock. This I had kept carefully secreted, as a last resort, to amuse the savages when other expedients should fail,—when memory and invention could yield no more tales, when promises should have become threadbare with repetition, and when pretensions of greatness at home should have lost their power by the every-day disclosure of present weakness and humiliation.

We—that is to say, myself and the old horse—kicked and floundered a while in the cold water, till at last the creature succeeded in rising, and I followed his example. We waded ashore, dripping, amidst the uproarious laughter of the whole troop. Once more mounted on my Rosinante, we resumed our line of march. The chill from my cold bath so benumbed me that I had to dismount and lead the horse, to recover, by brisk walking, some portion of animal warmth. Our course was down the river towards the Atlantic. Being unsuccessful in the chase, we pitched our tents at night, supperless, and without prospect of breakfasting the next morning. A small fire was lighted, which I hugged as closely as possible, to thaw my stiffened limbs; and then, cold, wet and hungry, fagged to extremity, cast myself on the ground, to repose as I might. The next morning was stormy. It cleared up in the afternoon, and the Indians sallied out to find some food. My only refreshment before their return was a little grease, which one of the squaws scooped out of an ostrich-skin with her dirty thumb and finger. It was so black that its pedigree—whether guanaco, ostrich or skunk, or a compound gathered at random from beast and bird—was a problem defying solution; but famine is not fastidious, and I swallowed greedily what, a few months before, I should hardly have thought fit to grease shoes with. The men came back with a few ostriches and skunks. The chief received as his portion one of the quadrupeds. The associations connected with its name, as related to one sense, were not adapted to prepossess the others in its favor; but I made shift to do justice rather to the Indian than to my habitual tastes.

During the three days we remained here, the long-concealed watch was brought to light. The filth of the natives, the condition in which their huts and their persons were always suffered to remain, the swarms of vermin they housed, had imposed upon me extraordinary care to prevent the natural results upon my own person; but no amount of precaution was sufficient to avert them. The reader will excuse me from speaking more particularly on this head. Enough to say that I found myself intolerably tormented. The chief ordered an examination of the case, and sent for an Indian to deal with it according to their art. While divesting myself of my garments, one by one, for this purpose, the old fellow caught sight of the hidden treasure. I knew that it was useless to attempt any longer to retain it, and handed it over. He was vastly pleased with it. I wound it up, and put it to his ear. He was as delighted at the unexpected sound as a child with its first rattle. I explained its use in keeping the hours of the day, but he cared for nothing but the ticking. The breaking of the crystal was explained, and he was informed that another should be procured as soon as we reached "Holland,"—another inducement, I hoped, to speed our passage there.

The inspection disclosed a state of the cuticle which would be thought dreadful in a civilized land. The chief, however, looked as calm as beseemed a surgical examiner, and in a good-natured guttural exchanged a few words with his assistant, who placed himself by my side, and fixing his eyes steadily upon me, begun swinging his hands and howling like a wild beast. The comparison was not far out of the way, for he gave a sudden spring, fastened his teeth on my neck, and commenced sucking the blood, growling all the while like a tiger! For a moment I thought my hour had come. I weaned the rascal as soon as possible, not knowing what his taste for blood might come to, if too freely indulged. It seemed like a refinement upon cannibalism, but was, in fact, as I soon ascertained, the regular treatment made and provided by Patagonian science for the relief of severe cutaneous affections.

The chief, all this while, recurred with undiminished pleasure to the ticking of his new toy. When his curiosity had at length abated, he returned it to me. I wrapped it carefully in a rag, and enveloped it afterwards in a young colt's skin provided for its reception, when, by direction of its present august proprietor, it was suspended among other valuables from one of the stakes of the hut, near the spot where his highness customarily reposed. It was not, however, allowed long to remain quiet. I was ordered to take it down and hold it to the ears of all the visitors to the lodge. Forty times a day it had to come down for this purpose, till I got so tired of my showman's duty that I wished the watch in the bottom of the sea. The Indians, as they listened to its vibrations, would stand in every attitude of silent amazement, their eyes dilated, their countenances lighted up in every feature with delighted wonder, and then break out in a roar of hoarse laughter, the tone of which strangely contrasted with the infantile simplicity of their demeanor. The business was dreadfully annoying, and yet it was plain that a new and almost unbounded power affecting my destiny was hidden in that little machine. It had captivated the chief, and struck an awe over the tribe like the rod of an enchanter. Whether it boded good or evil, was another question.

Our next move took us in a west-north-west direction, and in our progress we not only secured abundant game of the ordinary varieties, but encountered and killed a young lion,—to use the popular term,—the first living specimen I had seen in the country. I had seen their skins in possession of the Indians, and heard stories of their chase. This was a youthful creature, about the size of a well-grown calf of six weeks. I was riding side by side with the chief across a piece of low bushy land, when the dogs gave token that they scented something uncommon. We halted, and the chief cried out to the dogs, "Chew! Chew!" They were off in a jiffey, rushing hither and thither through the bushes, barking furiously, and soon drove the beast from his covert. Other Indians, a little distance off, ascertaining what was in the wind, made after the game with a reinforcement of dogs. The chase began in good earnest. Horses, riders and dogs, from all points of the compass, were scampering to the scene of action, hallooing, barking, howling, enough to frighten any unsophisticated lion out of his senses. Some were running full tilt, to cut off his retreat; while the hunters, bareheaded, leaning forward in their saddles and urging their horses to their utmost speed, whirled the bolas about their heads and let fly with a vengeance, with no other effect than to arrest the furious animal, and cause him to turn in desperation on the dogs, and drive them back yelping with pain. Others of the pack, watching their opportunity, would spring upon his back and fasten their teeth in his flesh. He brushed them off with a single stroke of his paw, as if they had been flies, and was again in motion, halting occasionally to give fight to his nearest assailant. Now and then the bolas is hurled at him, but his lithe limbs, though sometimes entangled, are not fettered by it, and his prowess is hardly diminished. The Indians press around him; the battle waxes fiercer; his whole strength is taxed. "Chew! Chew!" roar the savages; the flagging dogs return fresh to the onslaught, and, after a hard and unequal contest, the animal is fairly overborne by numbers, and despatched by the blows of the Indians. I had kept in the vicinity, but yet at a respectful distance, and now rode up to view the slain, amidst the howlings of the wounded dogs and the boisterous laughter of the hunters. It was a beautiful animal, with soft, sleek, silvery fur, tipped with black; the head having a general resemblance to that of a cat, the eye large and full, and sparkling with ferocity.

After the Indians had eyed their game sufficiently, and talked and laughed and grunted their satisfaction, and congratulated themselves generally on their victory, and severally on the part each had taken, the body was driven off on the back of a horse, and the hunters again spread themselves over the country. Some ostriches were soon started up. The chief drew out his bolas, put spurs to his horse, and darted away. His mantle fell from his shoulders: his long, straight black hair, so coarse that each particular hair stood independently on end, streamed in the wind; his hideously painted face and body loomed up with grotesque stateliness, and the deadly missile whirled frantically over his head. The whizzing weapon is suddenly hurled at his victim, the chief still sitting erect in his saddle to watch its effect. His horse suddenly stops,—he dismounts nimbly, seizes the entangled bird by the throat, and swings it violently around till its neck is broken. As I rode up he deposited the great bird on my horse, remounted, and rushed in pursuit of another. That was killed and also placed in my keeping, making me a kind of store-ship. Others pursue the guanaco with equal success, till they are satisfied with their booty. We ride up to a convenient thicket, a fire is lighted, a portion of the prey is cooked and eaten, the remnants of the feast and the residue of the game are duly packed up, and the whole troop is under march for the camp.

CHAPTER VI

The chief's oratory—A case of sickness novelly treated—The captive commissioned as physician to the chief—Dr. Bourne's first and last patient—Murder—Cannibalism—Another assassination, showing the perils of medical practice among savages—Sports of the children—Patagonian farriery—Slender success in the chase—A second struggle for life.

The chief occasionally made a speech to his subjects from the door of his lodge, wherein he invariably inculcated the duty of hunting industriously to procure meat, and a due supply of grease, for their families. He never had an auditor in sight, for his faithful lieges considered the speech from the throne a decided bore, and, if one happened to be passing, he was sure to dodge into the nearest hut till the infliction was over; but the leathern lungs of the orator could not fail to make him audible in many of the wigwams. In length his performances more resembled the official addresses of our republican rulers than those of his royal cousins of Europe, seldom falling short of a full hour. In style, they came nearer the proclamations of a crier. He would proceed in a monotonous rumble to the end of a sentence, and then defy contradiction by repeating several times, "Comole! comole! comole!" after which he paused, as for a reply. No one having the audacity to take up his challenge, he would go on croaking the same things with tedious iteration. After listening very patiently to one of his harangues, I inwardly applauded the taste of his subjects in getting as far as possible out of the reach of his voice.

One forenoon, as I was beginning to feel impatient to move,—for every movement seemed to fan the flickering hope that we would soon reach a place affording some avenue of escape, and this restlessness always made camp-life doubly dismal,—the chief informed me that we should decamp that day. Preparations had commenced, when one of his daughters came in with a child crying at a tempestuous rate. The version which she gave of his complaints arrested the marching orders. A messenger was forthwith despatched for one skilled in the healing art. The physician soon arrived, armed with two small packages rolled up in pieces of skin, about a foot long and three or four inches in diameter, which I took to be his medicine-chest. He walked gravely in, laid down the packages, and squatted beside the mother, who held the little patient in her arms. Whatever his ailment might have been, his lungs could not have been impaired, for he was roaring like a young buffalo. Not a word was spoken for some time, the doctor all the while looking him very steadily in the eye. Then came a sudden calm, importing that the little fellow experienced some relief, or, more probably, that he was exhausted. The doctor ordered an application,—not of hot water, according to the prescription of Sangrado, but of a mortar made of clay. The clay was brought, the anxious mother worked it over with her two hands, spitting upon it to give it the requisite moisture, and having reduced it to the consistency of thick paint, bedaubed the little fellow from head to foot, giving him a decidedly original appearance. He evidently took umbrage at this unction, and discoursed in his shrillest tones till he was fairly out of breath. The medicine-chests were opened, but, instead of medicinal herbs, disclosed only a bunch of ostrich's sinews and a rattle eight or ten inches long. The physician commenced fingering the strings, and muttering almost inaudibly. This lasted four or five minutes, at the expiration of which he seized his rattle, and clattered away furiously for a minute or two, and resumed his place by his patient, eying him intently as before. He then turned with an air of importance to the chief, who had been crouching cross-legged on his couch, leaning forward, with his arms tightly folded on his breast, and watching anxiously the progress of the treatment. The man of skill broke silence: "I think he is better; don't you?" The chief nodded, and grunted assent. The same appeal was made to the mother, and received a like response. Another plastering was ordered, another burst of melody followed the application, the mysterious strings were again fingered, duly followed by the rattle. The parent and grandparent once more assented to the leech that the child was better. The chief took out a piece of tobacco, and cut off enough for about two pipefuls, which was tendered and gratefully accepted as a professional fee. The strings were tied up and replaced in their proper receptacle, and the rattle was shaken with hearty good will, whether by way of finale to the cure, or as a note of gratitude for the fee, or of triumph for success, could not easily be guessed. But the practitioner had scarcely evacuated the lodge, before his patient broke out more vociferously than ever; which I thought would somewhat shake the faith of his guardians in the treatment he had received. But no; their confidence in their medical adviser was not to be blown away by a breath, or even a tempest. They evidently regarded him as nearly infallible. His remedies were obviously aimed more at the imaginations of his spectators than at the body of his patient, but it was no concern of mine. Patients among us have to endure more disagreeable applications than wet clay. The noisy brat became quiet, to our great relief. He shortly appeared to be quite well, and continued to thrive for some time, as I had opportunity to witness.

The tribe went ahead with alacrity, to make up for the loss of time this sickness occasioned. We moved off another day's journey towards nowhere in particular, and settled there at night. Then ensued another season of camp life, feasting and fasting, gambling and quarrelling, and venting superfluous wrath in an abundance of "Cashuran cashaly's." The chief was slightly indisposed, and I amused him with a description of the manner in which our physicians count the pulse of their patients. He listened with considerable interest, and sat thoughtfully ruminating on the matter. He came to an unexpected and alarming conclusion; putting this and my story of the opodeldoc together, he made up his mind that I was a physician myself! I protested against this inference, fearing that no good would come of the responsibilities he was inclined to impose on me. But the disclaimer was useless,—he stuck to the opinion; and in no long time it was understood through all the tribe that I was a distinguished doctor.

Now, it came to pass, at this critical turn of affairs, that a certain widow, of pretty ripe years for a Patagonian, was taken suddenly ill. Her husband had been murdered many years before by one of the tribe. She was possessed of several horses, and, in virtue of this wealth, held an aristocratic position in society. A messenger brought the tidings to the chief, who ordered me forthwith to set the watch, and go with him to her residence. I again assured him I knew nothing of sickness or medicine. He told me he knew better, and bade me come along without delay. There was no resisting his will, and I armed myself accordingly with the "ticking machine," and followed my master on my first professional visit. On approaching the widow's lodge, our ears were greeted with a hideous clamor, which momentarily increased as we neared the spot. A great crowd of Indians, of both sexes, surrounded the wigwam, severally and collectively making the most villanous noise ever heard. The crowd was dense, both within and without, but gave way for the chief and the great foreign physician to enter. The first order I gave was to stop their singing, whereat there was a silence so blank that the fall of a pin would have been audible,—that is, if there had been a floor for it to fall upon. With what dignity I could command, I walked up to my patient. There she lay, crouched on a bit of horse's skin, so withered, shrivelled and contracted, that it seemed as if a bushel-basket might have covered her, bed and all. I knelt by her side, drew forth the watch, grasped her by the wrist, and felt for her pulse. But, to my surprise, I could not feel it. I fussed and fumbled a long time, and finally arrived at the mortifying conclusion that I was so ignorant as not to know the position of the artery! The patient was frightened at so unprecedented a proceeding; but I succeeded in quieting her fears, though not, alas! in counting her pulse. However, it occurred to me that it was all one whether I did or not; so, keeping up an imperturbable gravity becoming my office, I continued for some time to look wisely at the watch, holding her wrist in profound silence. When I judged that a due impression had been produced on the awe-stricken spectators, I ventured to prescribe, not a clay plaster, for the patient was dirty enough, in all conscience; nor yet any compound of drugs, for I had none to administer; and as to roots and herbs, I durst not inflict upon her stomach substances of unknown properties; but, after a little thought, I ordered some water heated blood-warm, and the patient to be washed, and thoroughly scrubbed, from head to foot. This, I thought, met the most obvious indications of her case, as I doubt not a whole college of physicians, upon a superficial view, would have unanimously agreed. There could not have been a doubt as to the novelty of the prescription; the respectable relict, it is safe to say, had never been washed so thoroughly from infancy to that hour. Minute directions were given for the bath, that the scrubbing should be particularly smart and thorough. She was furthermore put upon a strict diet, excluding grease and all such luxuries, and we slowly retired from the sick room.

My solemnity was not affected,—far from it. Promotion from barber and showman to the dignity of physician to the chief, was too dangerous to be lightly considered. In fact, anxiety drove sleep from my eyes, and I fervently prayed for the recovery of the widow; fearing, from what I knew of the superstitions of the savages, that in case of her death I should be held responsible. In this particular case, as very soon appeared, I misjudged; but of the general principle I had startling confirmation.

The widow was better,—my prescription worked to a charm,—but her days were shortened. Late one night, after we had all retired to rest, a ferocious-looking rascal came into the chief's lodge; he muttered a few words to the chief, who arose, and went with him to the front of the wigwam. They conversed in a low tone several minutes, and separated, apparently with mutual satisfaction. I sounded the chief cautiously in reference to the matter in hand. Calmly, and without reserve, as if it were a very ordinary transaction, he said that the savages wished to kill the widow, in order to possess themselves of her horses, which they wanted to eat. I asked no further questions, being fully satisfied that he connived at the dark deed, which was consummated without delay. Before this tragic result, I had taken pains to disabuse the mind of the chief as to my supposed medical skill, and was able to relieve myself of the dangerous and burdensome honor.

Strange flesh was eaten by the Indians about this time; I was told it was lion-meat, but was not invited to partake of it. The same thing was observed several times; at times, too, when I was positive they had killed no wild animals without my knowledge, or which were not disposed of openly. The nature of my suspicions may be easily conjectured; yet I made no inquiries, in even the most casual manner, as to their disposition of their dead. It was painful to think of the atrocities, that were but too probably shrouded under the mystery they cast over these transactions. On one occasion, however, a young Indian, who could speak a few words of Spanish and English, told me that they had killed and eaten three men. Whether he meant to have me understand this as a singular case, or as a common action of the tribe, I do not know; I made no inquiries of him. In fact, the statement was volunteered by him; and so painful was the subject, that I left him abruptly, in the middle of a sentence.

We again moved in a north-westerly direction, taking a goodly quantity of game on the route, and settled in a wretched, marshy spot. The wind was high, and made the tents quiver like a ship in a gale; a storm set in, beating through the roofs, drenching and chilling me through all the night. On the evening of the second day of our encampment here, an incident occurred which fearfully confirmed the wisdom of my decision to renounce all title to medical skill. As I was seated by the dying embers of a little fire, surrounded by our motley household, and tugging manfully at a bit of half-raw meat, which constituted my evening meal, while a large piece was in process of cooking over the fire, we were suddenly startled by a cry of distress, followed by the distinct alarm of murder. The chief drew back to the rear of his lodge, took down his cutlass, and ordered me back from the fire, which was at once extinguished by two of his squaws, while the other two ran to the door, and set up a loud, lamentable wailing. All the women throughout the camp were, in like manner, giving their voices to the air, and "making night hideous;" and not a male Indian ventured to show his head for an hour or more. It was to me an hour of fearful suspense, the agony of which I cannot describe. At last a man came and told the chief that a doctor had been murdered. He had visited a woman professionally, and treated her case with charms and spells, but his prescriptions effected no satisfactory result; and her husband went in a rage to his lodge, and stabbed him with repeated blows, to make the work of death more sure. It was a singular circumstance, that men capable of deliberate murder, and who had so recently, with the tacit or open sanction of the chief, strangled a woman for her horses, should have shown so much alarm at the cry of murder on this occasion. The victim was an enormously fat man, weighing, I should judge, nearly four hundred pounds. A horrible sight presented itself the next morning, on going out of our hut; the snow around the doctor's lodge was saturated with his blood. I drew back from the sickening spectacle, unable to look upon it with composure. Beyond their exhibition of stupid terror in the night, no notice was taken of the act; and about noon the camp broke up. We travelled till night, meeting with no success in the chase, and encamped on an extensive plain, near a good spring of water.

It was an occasional diversion to watch the children at their sports, of which a favorite one was throwing ostriches' feet, with the sinews of the legs attached. The toes are cut off, and a pair of the feet are tied together, with a piece of sinew about a yard long. The children begin to practise the sport as soon as they are able to walk, and will continue the amusement all day; one boy throwing them into the air, and others throwing and hitting them as they fly, therein serving an apprenticeship to the grand manly accomplishment of hurling the bolas. Young Cohanaco, the chief's youngest son, appeared to excel all others; he was looked upon as a remarkably smart and very active lad; and, though he was six or eight years old, was not yet weaned! All the tribe fondled and caressed him; he would practise with the boys, often without any covering to his back, till excited and almost exhausted; then he would run into the lodge, take refreshment at his mother's breast, and speedily return to his sport.

All this time Holland was not forgotten, but the chief and his lieges were continually reminded of the urgent reasons for taking me there without delay; the presents which could only be obtained there, the fearful consequences of suffering me to come to harm, the great ships with the big guns, &c. &c., that would assuredly avenge me upon the whole tribe,—with what effect, beyond allaying present irritations and discontents that threatened me, it was impossible to determine.

A novel sample of farriery offered itself to my observation one day, while hunting with the chief; my old horse, on a sudden, began to hobble, and very nearly gave out. I watched him some time, and jolted on, suffering somewhat from his uneven movements, but could not discern the occasion of the difficulty. On dismounting and examining his feet, nothing serious was perceptible, except that the hoofs were worse for wear, and broomed up a little. I remounted, and gave the poor creature a smart drubbing, to overtake his owner, if possible, and consult him on the case, which was one wherein I was content to defer to his wiser judgment. Sufficient steam was raised to bring us abreast of the chief, who, on hearing what was the matter, put spurs to his horse, and told me to come on—"Bueno caballo, se campo, campo." I tried to comply, but it was hard starting the beast, though I used up considerable wood to that end. The chief having got far in advance, and finding me desperately in arrears, hove to, and waited for me. I toiled on, and succeeded in working a passage to his position. He dismounted, inspected the horse's feet, and, directing me to wait his return, rode off. He soon reäppeared with a piece of guanaco-skin, which he tied securely about the hoof of the lame foot. I expressed some surprise at this method of shoeing horses; but he said, "Buenos zapatos,"—good shoes,—and the event confirmed his words. The lameness nearly disappeared, and we jogged on together without any further trouble.

While at this camping-ground, the chief one morning arose in a towering passion at some words let fall by one of his wives, and exhibited another sample of the rigor of matrimonial discipline, very similar to that which graced the nuptials of his daughter. He gave her a tremendous beating, which seemed enough to kill her outright; but she took it very calmly, as a sort of necessary evil incident to the married state.

Once more on the move, the squaws taking charge of the furniture and baggage, including the pappooses, and the men riding in advance as usual, to chase supplies for the larder. Game was scarce; we got a couple of ostriches and a skunk,—or a couple of skunks and an ostrich, I forget which, and it makes less difference to the reader than at the time it did to me. We cooked and lunched on the ground, and turned our faces homeward with the scanty remainder. The women were busy erecting the wigwams. The ground was frozen, and a large iron bolt, doubtless from some wreck, served as a crowbar to dig holes for the stakes. The encampment was on a hill-side, near a low swamp, which furnished abundance of water, such as it was.

We had scarcely settled down, and I was dreading the stagnant monotony of camp life, when dulness was dispelled in a most unwelcome manner. Knots of Indians could be seen in murmuring conversation, whose glances betrayed the bent of their passions. They were again getting impatient of my life, and caresses and flattery were of no avail to stem the rising tide. On the evening of the third day, I was summoned out of the lodge by the chief, and followed him in silence, with a trembling presentiment of evil. He led me to a spot where twenty or thirty leading spirits in the tribe sat ranged in a circle,—the fatal ring was once more set to ensnare me! Once I had escaped. Was it possible to effect a second escape? Everything said no. The chances seemed a hundred to one against it. What had I left unsaid, to tempt their cupidity, to excite alarm, to make them value my safety or dread the effects of harming me? I could think of nothing, and the dismal prospect benumbed every faculty of my soul. But, as I entered the ominous circle, an access of fresh strength, the courage of desperation, enabled me to bear up with energy against perplexity and fear; to resolve that I would meet them with a steadfast eye and an inflexible mind,—a force which, though springing out of weakness, should prove stronger than their utmost malice.

Having seated myself near the chief, the consultation began and proceeded much as before, but with increased vehemence. Their demonstrations were alarming, but, to my joy, the chief took the same view as in the former council. Would he be able to restrain their savage tempers? His power was great, but there was a limit to its effect, and I feared. In my turn I sought to enforce his views, by arraying all the motives invention could produce, and was able to perceive that they had some weight. Again the matter was canvassed around the ring. There was a hesitation, as if they felt suspicious and unsatisfied. Then they began to cross-examine me; my promises were not explicit enough. What did I mean to give them? The answer did not content them; they wanted more. More or less made no difference to me, and I gave them assurance of all the good things they craved, when we should arrive at Holland. Another talk followed, and brought them to a pretty unanimous conclusion, that they would get the presents first, and decide my fate afterwards;—a "squeeze-your-orange-and-throw-it-away" policy, in which these rascals seemed to be remarkable adepts.

The natives had no idea that I could understand their talk, and I was not at all eager to display my acquisitions. In fact, though unable to speak their jargon, my ear had become pretty well trained to interpret it, while my scraps of half Spanish enabled me, without suspicion, to hear, mark and digest, much of their conversation. This was, in part, acquired in teaching some of them, the youth especially, to speak English and to count,—a pursuit in which I engaged partly for their benefit, and partly for my own. Besides aiding me in learning their language, it tended, so far as it diverted their attention, to keep mischief out of their heads, after the manner in which constant employment maintains order in a ship's crew. It added to my knowledge of their character and ways of thinking, so that, in dangerous emergencies, I was able to detect the first symptoms of evil. More than once it enabled me to elude or to nip in the bud dangerous conspiracies, which, if they had gone further, might have proved fatal to me. Circumspection made self-possession more easy. I will confess—though the narrative may have made confession needless—that I am naturally timid, and inclined to the better part of valor. Yet somehow—God helping me—I early learned to hide my constitutional timidity under a show of fearlessness, even in circumstances of great peril. More than once, when a savage drew his knife at me, have I looked him in the eye and disarmed him by a laugh; perhaps laying hold of the instrument of death, trying its edge and praising its qualities, till its owner was shamed into quiet. One piece of English that tickled the chief was the title of "Old Boy," with which (from a conviction of its appropriateness) I early honored him, and which he appeared to relish as much as if I had called him "His Majesty."

The council, to my great relief, at length broke up, and I returned to my wretched shelter. The chief pointed to my bed, and bade me lie down. I complied, not to sleep, but to adore the Providence that had twice rescued me as from the very jaws of death, to reflect on the past and to speculate on the future. The excitement of the evening kept me wakeful, and the night wore away and the morning dawned, without sleep for a moment visiting my eyes.

CHAPTER VII

A new torture—Bloody gossip—An explosion nearly fatal—Plea of insanity—Reconciliation—River Santa Cruz—Naval architecture—Original mode of ferrying—Accident—Ominous demonstrations thereupon—Perilous superstition—Plans of escape—The chief fighting his battles over again—Prospects brighten—A blind hint to naturalists.

From this point we moved again in a north-westerly direction, finding game more plenty, and among other animals captured a species of fox, the first I had seen in the country. The camping-ground selected was a waste more desolate than had yet greeted my sight, even in Patagonia,—a low marsh, surrounded by sand-hills destitute of even the semblance or vestige of vegetation, past or present. The horses were let loose to solve the problem of existence as they could, while my landladies, with their canine assistants, served up a skunk and two ostrich-legs for supper. I thought myself fortunate at getting so ample a meal, having been on short allowance the preceding day.

Here a new torture was inflicted. There had been abundance of voluble hatred against me, as I had too good reason to know, but it was around and behind me. Now, presuming, doubtless, on my ignorance of their language, they came to utter their bloodthirsty thoughts in my presence. At night, before retiring, the women began to talk against me, as usual; which never gave me much uneasiness, female opinion not having much force, I suspected, in affairs of state. Two of them had always appeared to bear me a mortal grudge, for what cause I could not conjecture, unless they thought I took up too much of his highness' time, or exerted too much influence over him. But, on the present occasion, the conference was enlarged by the entrance of two or three visitors, whose only errand seemed to be to give the chief gratuitous advice touching the disposal of my person. Though perfectly comprehending the drift of their remarks, I looked as stupid as possible, and bent myself to caress and flatter the old fellow with more than common servility;—patting his breast, telling him what a big, good heart it contained, calling him my compadre, and myself his child, his piconine, his muchacho. So deep was my abasement! To talk of the goodness of a heart beating with cruelty and black with crime! To call that black, greasy, depraved monster my father, and myself his dutiful and affectionate son! It is humiliating to speak of this;—what, let the reader imagine, must it have been to feel it! The bruised reed was well-nigh broken. The courage that sustained me in sharp trials was frittered away piecemeal by incessant irritation. Hope, that kept me from fainting in the fatal ring, vanished with the occasion that invoked it, and a bitter, consuming despair hovered over me. Then came dark and distracting thoughts of home, now more distant than ever, to stab my heart, already faint and bleeding. Again was sleep driven from me, but the night passed, and the blessed light of day stole upon me, as with a benediction from heaven.

I arose and rushed into the open air to warm myself by exercise, and when the fire was lighted comforted myself by its kindly heat, and recovered a measure of buoyancy. But the day was wearily spent, and night brought the merciless gossips once more into the lodge. The two squaws led off with words of the most fiendish hate, urging that I should be summarily despatched, and gloating over anticipated vengeance. Tempestuous thoughts and sleepless hours had weakened me in body and mind. The fall of successive drops of water will madden the stoutest brain, and the drop too much had now lighted on my head. I was frenzied; strong passions, hitherto held in check, overmastered me. I rose, threw my cap violently on the ground, stamped, gnashed my teeth, and cursed without restraint. I shook my fists at them, defied their malice, and raved for several minutes, reckless of consequences. What was life to me? They were killing me by inches. Let them do their worst, no matter how soon. The chief was at first startled at such an explosion, and sat looking fixedly upon me, with a dark and clouded brow. It was fortunate that my rage was too impetuous to be contained within the bounds of my Indian-Spanish vocabulary, but breathed itself in good strong Saxon, so that speech could not betray me. For no sooner had the internal pressure been measurably relieved, than a sudden consciousness of error—fatal error—smote me with a new dread. What had I done? Where were my wits, that I should toss away life to gratify impotent anger? If my chance of life was worth little to myself, was it worth nothing to others, that I should so trifle with it? With returning sanity of feeling came also a hint of the way to repair my wrong. Without waiting for any questions or wordy explanations, I looked piteously at the chief, pointed to my head, and assured him it was disordered. I could not help my actions. I was sorry to make such an exhibition of myself, but it was all my poor head; and holding on to the poor head with one hand, I beat it reproachfully with the other, at the same time giving vent to some unearthly noises by way of corroboration. The old fellow looked rather dubiously at this change of scene, and asked if it was at them I shook my fists?—At them? No, no! they did not understand me. My heart was good, like his, but it was all my head, my poor naughty cabeza. Another thump on my cranium, and a second edition of the howl, proved sufficient. The plea of insanity was admitted; he expressed himself satisfied, and explained the incident to the amazed spectators. I drew a long breath with a returning sense of security, scarcely crediting the success of the artifice, and almost doubting whether the whole scene were not a dream. Real or unreal, it was over, and things were apparently on their former footing. Only my feminine foes would not be convinced, and added this crowning indiscretion to the list of my offences.

We moved the next day in a northerly direction, and struck the river Santa Cruz, encamping about an eighth of a mile from its marshy banks, which, at this point, were bent in a broad, horse-shoe curve. We were surrounded, except on the river side, by high abrupt sand-banks, covered in part by underbrush of a stunted growth. The river was narrow, but deep and rapid. The Indians said it was the Santa Cruz, and that it led directly to "Holland;" but their lies about that same Dutch land had long since destroyed all faith in their words. That it was the Santa Cruz was probable, for I knew of no other river in these parts;—we had passed Corey Inlet and the Gallegos. The rest of the story I could only try to credit. I tried to urge them on, but they were not to be hurried. Some of them grumbled that I had no intention of giving them anything, but meant to slip from them the first opportunity. No wonder they thought so; they certainly had not laid me under very great obligations of gratitude. What on earth they wanted of me, unless to fat and eat me, was past conjecture; and my fare had not been of a nature to induce corpulence, so that this supposition was not trustworthy. They said they wanted me to help steal horses. They were bound for the Rio Negro, where they meant to steal seven hundred horses, of which number I was to get two. Certainly, I told them, it would be just the thing; and that was a most excellent reason for going to "Holland." They would find me a rare thief; but, however it might be with them, I could not steal without a good stock of rum and tobacco. Was I insincere in all this? The reader may smile or may frown, but it was my purpose, if I failed to escape by way of "Holland," to humor them to the top of their bent; to ride, hunt, and even steal my way into their confidence;—any way to insure present safety, and keep an eye open for future opportunities.

Three or four days were passed in suspense, which was at last terminated by taking our line of march down the river. We halted at noon, at a point where the banks sloped gently to the water's edge, on either side of the deep and narrow channel. Active preparations were here commenced for crossing. Part of the horses were driven across the river, whilst a portion of the tribe were occupied in building boats to ferry their families and goods across. Their boats are constructed after a simple fashion. A quantity of bushes are cut and dragged down to the margin of the water. They take four tent-stakes, and lay them so as to enclose an area eight feet square, lashing them firmly together at the four corners. Four Indians then raise the stakes from the ground, while others place the skin covering of the tent over the frame, allowing it to sag down three or four feet. The edges of the skin are brought over the stakes, and fastened on the inside. The bushes, made ready for the purpose, are placed within, tops downward, round the entire circumference, and secured to the stakes, till the boat is completely timbered up. The bushes keep the skin distended, and give to the vessel an oval shape, so that, though square at the top, it bears a striking resemblance to a large iron pot. Its length and its breadth of beam are of course equal. When completed, it is firmly lashed from stem to sternpost, and from side to side, with a lariat, or green hide rope, forty feet long, to keep it from spreading or racking. I had no hand in modelling this witch of the wave, but, like an apprentice, did as I was ordered in forwarding the structure, and, when nothing else was required, "held on to the slack." It was at last completed, like the temple of Solomon, without the sound of axe or hammer; neither bolts, trenails nor caulking-iron, were required. We carried the barge down, and launched her in the stream. Two paddles were made by lashing two bladebones of the guanaco to sticks. Squaws, pappooses and baggage, were stowed away, till the boat was laden to the water's edge. I was directed to take passage with the family and household effects of the chief, and seated myself in the centre of the closely-packed craft. One end of a lariat was fastened to the boat, and the other tied to the tail of a horse. A savage mounted, with one rein attached to the wooden bit on the up-stream side. Two others took the oars, one on each side, and a squaw was stationed on the top-gallant forecastle for the purpose of singing, to insure good luck. All is ready. The old horse wades till the depth of water compels him to swim, and the boat is pushed off. The rider floats on the horse's back, kicking the water with his feet, holding the rein in one hand, and grasping the mane with the other. "Chew! chew!" he shouts, at the top of his voice. The black swan in the forecastle opens her capacious mouth and sings, "Yek yah, youri miti! yek yah, youri miti!" The two oarsmen dig away with might and main, while the younger fry swell the chorus with a "Yah! yah! yah!" The boat brings some heavy lurches to the windward, then yaws off to leeward; all owing to those lubberly oarsmen not meeting her with the helm in season. At length, after innumerable shiftings, we reached the opposite shore, and waded up on dry land.

FERRYING THE SANTA CRUZ

Several boats were constructed after the same unique model, and succeeded in crossing safely. Some of the horses, being better adapted to towing, were swam back to repeat the process, and our craft returned for a second freight. I watched the proceedings from the bank with intense interest, speculating on the probable consequences of an accident to any of the fleet. Such was their superstition, that, in the event of any ill befalling them, they would be quite likely to ascribe it to me, and serve me worse than Jonah was treated by his shipmates. The swiftness of the current, and the rudeness of their navigation, made them so liable to mischief, that it seemed wise to prepare for it; and I at once began ingratiating myself with two of the worst fellows in the whole tribe, by professions of special good will and admiration for them, and confidential hints that they would share more liberally in the bounties of "Holland" than any of their fellows. Whilst thus engaged, with cautious glances across the river, to make sure that all was right, I perceived that there was quite a commotion among the people below; some were springing upon their horses,—others, ready mounted, were dashing furiously down the bank. On looking some distance below, a boat appeared to be in distress; the lariat that bound it together had snapped asunder, and the pressure within, and the strain of the horse without, had broken the front stake; the horse, relieved of his freight, pulled for the shore, and could neither be coaxed nor beaten into a return to duty. The horsemen on the banks dashed into the stream, and swam for the wreck, which contained, among other passengers, a young child. It was already filled with water, and was partially turned on her side. The surface of the river was dotted with dark forms, struggling with the mad current; one horseman after another each grasped a floating object, and made for the shore. The craft had drifted nearly half a mile, and nothing could be made out very distinctly. The squaws, on first perceiving the mischance, watched the wreck, and sung in a loud and plaintive strain, all the while casting unfriendly glances at me, and gradually approaching the place where I stood. My apprehensions were so far confirmed by this movement, that I told John (the name I gave one of my present particular friends), as he loved rum and tobacco, and expected to get any, not to leave me. John saw at a glance what was in the wind, and appreciated both the immediate danger and the ultimate reward of averting it; namely, the privilege of being gloriously drunk at my expense. He told me to go into his hut, and pointed me to the furthest corner; where, I being duly ensconced, he took his station, cutlass in hand, directly in front of me. The singing grew louder, and the voices more numerous about the door; the song was their regular powwow strain, which invariably preluded the killing of a horse. The Indians began to enter the lodge, and looked unutterable things in the direction where I was crouching; the wigwam was soon filled with them, and they were beginning to crowd towards me, when old John opened upon them, and told them they ought to be ashamed of themselves, to come in there in that manner; they did not even know what had happened,—they did not know whether any lives were lost. They were threatening on account of the death of a child, when, for aught they knew, the child was alive; they had better wait patiently, till they knew more about the matter, before they made any further uproar about it. In this strain he parleyed with them for some time, till they concluded to retire, uttering, as they went, the most horrible sounds. I felt less relief from their absence than if John had not, by implication, fully assented that if the brat was drowned, my life should answer for it. News soon came that the children were all safe, but that the boat was lost.

An instant change ensued: the fire appeared to be quenched, but I feared it might break out at any moment afresh. Knowing their treachery, I kept a pretty suspicious watch on their movements; the chief soon came over the river, hurried, perhaps, in his movements by the accident, which he had witnessed from the opposite shore. After conferring with John, and giving him some instructions, and seeing that all was right, he reëmbarked for the other shore, as he made it his special business to see that all were passed across in safety. The ferrying ceased as night came on; the chief was likely to be on the opposite side all night, as there was a good day's work yet to be done before the whole would be transported. I had overheard him giving special orders to keep a good look-out on me during the night. I felt, however, some uneasiness in his absence; he had been my most powerful protector, having twice, at least, saved me from imminent death.

I now began to revolve in my mind the possibility of escape; the thought suggested itself that I might steal one of their boats, and drift down the stream. I was long since heartily tired of captivity; my situation, especially if I was to be held a hostage of Providence for the safe ferriage of the tribe, was desperate. But, on second thought, I did not know that this was certainly the Santa Cruz; if it was, I was furthermore ignorant of our distance from the sea. I knew of no white settlement on or near the river; none, I remembered, was laid down in the chart; if such a settlement existed, I might hope to reach it in a boat, but a voyage in such a craft as one of these would be as hazardous as that of the wise men of Gotham. If there was no such settlement, and "Holland" was Patagonian for Utopia, my only chance, short of drifting in my leathern sack out to sea, would be to land on some island, in case an island there were; and then what should I live on, after landing? Berries I had never seen, except once or twice. Besides, my stolen craft could not be paddled,—the Indians had too good ears for that; I must follow the channel passively, through all its course, which was terribly crooked, while its rapidity increased the risk that the ungainly vehicle would be disabled. On the whole, it was so doubtful whether I could reach any particular place, or escape starvation after I got there, and so certain that failure would be death, the project seemed a forlorn hope. But then, again, it was not more forlorn than my present situation; so my poor mind vibrated between dangers,—the danger of remaining where I was,—the danger that I should escape only from the frying-pan into the fire. At last, as I felt the frying-pan, and only feared the fire, I concluded to try.

Crawling as noiselessly as possible from my resting-place, I stole softly out, and made for the river. Alack! in calculating the chances, I had not once thought of four-footed enemies, and they were upon me before I was halfway to the shore,—a half-dozen dogs, barking loud enough to wake the whole encampment. I retreated incontinently to the lodge, and succeeded in getting quietly into my quarters again, not without some inward spasms. It was all for the best, no doubt, but it was not, just then, easy to think so, or possible to feel so; and, therefore, after a little time, I once more emerged from the lodge, and stole towards the river by a different track, hoping to elude those infernal dogs; but they, or some others, were on the alert, and came pell-mell upon my rear, barking more uproariously than before. I cursed the dogs, their masters, and my own folly, and gave up the attempt.

The ferrying recommenced the next morning; and before night the whole tribe were safely landed, with their effects, on the west side of the river, and their wigwams were all pitched. We were short of provisions; but this was a common case, and I was accustomed to it. I got an occasional morsel of grease, sufficient to keep starvation at bay; but illness, with bad and insufficient food, had greatly emaciated me, till I was a spectacle but few degrees above the living skeleton. But hope was still in the ascendant, and I had no idea of lying down to die till I was quite sure my time had come. We continued our wanderings the next day in a westerly direction, slaying every living creature that came within reach, from a skunk to a guanaco. This was a great disappointment, as I hoped we should go down the river, the direction in which they said "Holland" lay, and the only direction in which we were likely to strike a white settlement, if any existed on the Atlantic coast. But my remonstrances on this head were vain; they would go where they pleased, and I must go with them. Time dragged heavily; hours seemed days, and days weeks. But impatience is no virtue, and submission was imperative.

The country hereabout was more broken and mountainous than any we had before traversed, with a more abundant growth of bushes, and some clumps of stunted trees here and there. As we proceeded, keeping still to the north-west, game was more plenty. We came to two ponds, or small lakes, one of not more than four acres in extent, the other considerably larger; the latter was shallow, at least near the shore, as some ostriches pursued by the Indians ran into it, and their pursuers waded after, and succeeded in capturing them.

At one time I observed a large scar in the calf of the chief's leg; the mark of a wound that must have been inflicted a long time before, as it was completely healed. Its depression was so great as to indicate a very severe cut, unless the old fellow had grown uncommonly fat since he received it. On inquiring the cause of it, he said it was from a wound inflicted by the Alanagros, a tribe inhabiting a country to the northward. The name he gave them signifies the blacks; and, from the manner in which he spoke of them, I inferred they were in some respects superior to the Patagonians. He said they were armed with cutlasses, and very long knives,—had tobacco, and plenty of horses; and I conjectured that they might have been a party of Spanish Americans, or one of the mixed races of Spanish origin. The fight, he said, arose on occasion of his tribe being on a horse-stealing expedition; they encamped a short distance off, and at night he made a descent on the Alanagros, killed some of them, and plundered their camp, carrying off many of their horses. The plundered tribe rallied, hotly pursued them, and recaptured a part of the booty; in the struggle wounding him with a cutlass, and, as I judged by appearances, cutting to the bone. He told the story with great spirit, slashing right and left, and grunting with extraordinary emphasis, as if to give an impression that good hard blows were given and taken: but I afterwards learned that it was a cowardly running fight, in which more sweat than blood was spilled.

Nothing of importance occurred at our encampment near the lakes, except—what was a very noteworthy fact with me—such an abundance of ostrich that I was surfeited with the delicious fare, and was compelled by the chief to take a horse-rein emetic,—a more precise description of which the reader will have no difficulty in excusing. Had I not so completely disavowed the medical character, the chief might probably have allowed me to feel my own pulse,—if I could find it,—and to prescribe for myself; but the renunciation of professional honors brought me under the sanitary, as well as the political, jurisdiction of Parosilver.

Our line of march was now in a northerly direction, soon deflecting to the eastward,—a movement that revived my sinking hopes. There seemed to be some prospect of striking the Atlantic coast, and coming within reach of civilized men. On our way we observed the tracks of some animals different from any I had met with. The chief said it was the limerer, with which lucid definition I was fain to be content; and, as no specimens were visible, the inquisitive naturalist must trust to his imagination for the rest.

CHAPTER VIII

Retrograde march—A look-out ahead—New specimens of birds observed—To the right again—Large inducements to visit Holland—Apparent effect—Council—Other tribes of Indians—Story of a battle—Capture of wild horses—A royal speech worth hearing—Deputation to Holland—A start and a sudden halt—Journey commenced in earnest—Order of arrangements—First view of Holland—A weary day and night—A boat—A short parley—Swimming for life and liberty—A rescue—Farewell to Patagonia.

My hopes were soon cast down, by a decided movement to the westward. Every step, I was convinced, lengthened the distance between me and the spot where my most earnest wishes centred; for, though I knew not of any settlements in this barren region, yet it was pretty certain that if there was one it must be sought in the line of the Santa Cruz. Of our latitude and longitude I could form no decisive judgment; but by the aid of the sun, of which occasional glimpses were caught, it was easy to take note of our direction, and I never retired to rest without taking landmarks, and satisfying myself as nearly as possible as to our whereabouts. At night there was a renewal of the discussions which had once so nearly turned my brain, and now at times came near verifying the plea which then saved me from destruction; but I was enabled to keep my feelings in more equal check. Disappointed and care-worn, I spent the night in commending myself to the mercy and good providence of God, praying that he would soften the heart of the savage and open a way of deliverance.

Among other matters that excited my curiosity, I was anxious to know whether the Indians were expert swimmers. The only occasion on which I had seen them attempt it was at the time of the accident in crossing the river. Then two of them swam across, while the others floated on their horses' backs, clinging to the mane. In answer to some questions dropped on the subject, the chief assured me that they were all expert swimmers, and could stretch off a long distance without resting, as they would show me, but that the coldness of the season made the experiment too unpleasant. Others of the tribe told the same story. The question was interesting, for obvious reasons. I had thought a time might come when it would be a very practical one.

Some new specimens of birds made their appearance from time to time. One was a large black bird, resembling the turkey-buzzard, and subsisting on carrion. Another resembled the snow-birds of the north. I had also seen, near the sea-shore and by the lakes, several species of water-fowl,—one not unlike the wild goose, but the chief said they were not good for food.

Our course, the next day, was northward, and the day following turned once more decidedly towards the east, whereat my hopes, varying with the compass, began to revive, though their buoyancy was tempered by experience of the uncertainty of Indian movements. Observing a spot covered with small trees, over which a great number of carrion birds hovered, we approached and found the carcass of a poor old guanaco, which had most likely paid the debt of nature without compulsion, and was stripped of its flesh by the birds. The chief broke some of the bones and eagerly sucked the marrow, and then picked up the remainder to add to the domestic stock of grease.

At the close of the next day we brought up at a ravine, and found our camp by following it a short distance to a low flat. Proceeding to the eastward all the next day, we ascended a high eminence, from which the chief pointed in a south-westerly direction, and said that "Holland" lay there. I strained my eyes in the quarter indicated, without, however, making any discoveries, and with a strong disposition to think the Old Boy was hoaxing me. At dark we defiled down a steep declivity, and pitched our tents on the border of an extensive marsh covered with ice. Here I renewed my arguments for speeding our way to the promised land, dilating on the qualities of the promised rum in a style that would have astonished the advocates of the Maine liquor law, and impaired the confidence of those who had reasonably regarded me as a strict temperance man. Indeed, the antics and grimace with which I enforced the description, and illustrated the jovial effects of the creature,—the boasts of how I would teach them, by its aid, to throw the lasso, and perform most astonishing feats of horse-stealing and riding,—might have induced a suspicion that I knew more of it than mere observation or fancy could teach. But, however it may affect my reader, it produced unmistakable contentment and satisfaction to my Patagonian auditors; and that was what I aimed at. They looked and listened with watering mouths and hoarse laughter, giving token that the balmy description was appreciated to a most desirable degree. So evident was the impression that I spent the next day running about and giving line upon line to the most influential of the tribe, and succeeded, as I thought, in awakening a degree of enthusiasm to move towards the place where all these good things were to be got. In confirmation of this, I had the satisfaction of being called at night to attend a solemn council.

It was a peaceful gathering,—they left their weapons behind,—but it contemplated only a sort of preliminary inquiry; the Patagonians know how to make their forms of procedure as tedious as any of our courts of law, summary as are many of their dealings. They examined and cross-examined very strictly, sifting my story with a severity which showed that they were in earnest, and at the same time a little suspicious. It was necessary to be on my guard at all points; and if they had been more docile learners of arithmetic, and able to stick on questions of number and quantity, it might have been a harder matter to satisfy them. But, on the whole, the old story was stuck to with a degree of consistency that produced the desired effect. Their confidence was perceptibly raised, and, after a good deal of talk, the council adjourned, every one more than ever disposed to visit "Holland."

While at this encampment, I observed on the ground about a dozen large oyster-shells, that appeared to have been recently opened. These were the first and only shells of the kind I saw in the country. I inquired if they were plenty in that vicinity. They said they were not; none of the tribe seemed to know where they came from, or anything about them. The chief said that he and his people did not relish oysters, but other Indians ate them. He did not like fish of any kind; no fish had grease enough for them; none of his Indians ate fish. This, and some similar incidents and conversations, convinced me that there were other Indian tribes in the vicinity. On one occasion I had noticed some places where a tribe, probably as numerous as our own, had encamped. Their fires appeared to have been very recently extinguished. Our tribe appeared to be considerably disturbed at these discoveries, and I judged that they were the traces of some enemies. It is certain that my captors had seen some desperate fights, of which they bore the marks on their persons. One of them had a deep scar on his breast, which he said was the mark of an arrow-shot received from the "Yamaschoner" Indians, a tribe that use the bow and arrow. His description suggested the probability that these were the Terra-del-Fuego Indians; but, on mentioning the conjecture at a later period to a person I met at the Chilian penal settlement, he informed me that those islanders invariably shoot poisoned arrows, which would not leave the victim much leisure to describe their effect. The scar in question was a deep one, in the region of the heart; and while I was examining it, the chief remarked that the arrow passed through his body and came out at his back. On examination, a distinct scar was visible on his back, so far corresponding in form and direction with the one in front, that it seemed likely to have been made by the same weapon. But how the arrow could have transfixed him through the chest, without wounding the vital organs, was not easily to be conjectured. The only explanation I could conceive of was, that the fellow's heart was so much harder than any material used for arrowheads, that the missile, instead of penetrating that important organ, had glanced aside and passed without mortal hurt. Enough had been developed to assure me that the tribe generally had hearts of no ordinary toughness, capable of serving them for all practical purposes wherein impenetrable stuff was in request; but the tale of this miraculous escape gave a new impression of obduracy, and entitled the hero to bear the palm among his fellows. I pretended to pity him for his former sufferings, and went so far as to volunteer—in case I should ever be permitted to enter the enemy's territory—to make mince-meat of some of them, and so to avenge his cruel injuries. This spontaneous sympathy and forwardness to take up his quarrel was exceedingly gratifying to the sufferer and to the chief, and drew from them a more particular narrative of the combat.

They were out on a horse-stealing expedition,—the usual occasion, it seems, of Patagonian fights,—and made a swoop upon the camp of another tribe. The objects of this felonious invasion asserted title to the horses in their possession by certain tangible arguments, and induced a mortal combat. And now Old Boy waxed eloquent, and especially displayed that prime ingredient, "action." His broad-sword exercise was really animated, and taught us "how fields were won,"—or would have done so, but that, while his right hand was slashing the air with his good steel, his left would hold the bridle-rein, and his heels involuntarily drive the spur;—in short, though it was a part on which he did not linger in the narration any more than in the act, there was some tall running on the occasion. So artlessly was the tale told, that while the hero was cutting and thrusting and grunting, to make due impression of the desperate bravery displayed in the encounter, his subordinate action clearly depicted a running and retreating fight, and convinced me that they got a sound drubbing for their pains. He said he killed one Indian, with an air that would have done justice to the slaying of a regiment. Shocking to relate, there were found persons who slanderously reported to me that Old Boy's legs had the unhappy propensity of Pat O'Flaherty's, whose heart was as brave as any man's, but his cowardly legs ran away with his body; and they scrupled not to affirm that in this same hard-fought battle he crawled into the bushes, and there secreted himself till the cessation of hostilities enabled him to rejoin his tribe.

The reader has doubtless noticed that "the tribe" has been all along anonymous. The explanation comes rather late, but, in point of fact, I never could learn that they had any distinctive name; they never used any. Indeed proper names were very seldom heard. Even in conversation concerning each other, they managed to avoid "naming names" as strictly as so many honorable senators, though for no reason that I could discover. By signs and gestures, and other hints, they indicated the personal subject of remark, and seemed to suffer no inconvenience from what would be felt among us as a serious want.

While out hunting one day with the chief, we ascended a slight eminence, commanding a view of an extensive plain. The chief suddenly stopped his horse, and looked steadily forward. I bent my eyes in the same direction, and saw two or three mounted Indians moving towards a common point. There was nothing unusual to be seen, but Old Boy seemed to discover something. I inquired what it was. He answered by pointing; and, on a second view, I observed a horse loose, which I took to be that of some Indian temporarily dismounted. But the chief said they were about to catch a wild horse, and forthwith dashed off at a furious rate, bidding me follow. We were rapidly nearing the spot, when the two in advance of us put their horses at top speed towards the lone horse that was standing beside a clump of bushes. It suddenly ran before its pursuers, followed by two colts from the thicket. The colts appeared to be one or two years old, and were doubtless following their dam. One Indian singled out the mare, and another the larger colt. The little one did not lag behind. The chief and myself followed at a pace which would have made a single misstep fatal to our necks; but fortunately our horses proved sure-footed. On we dashed, helter-skelter, in a direction to head off the pursuers, and to place ourselves nearest to the affrighted animals. The mare yet holds the lead, and fairly tears up the soil with her flashing hoofs. An Indian, in close pursuit, presently swings his lariat about his head; but she makes a curve in her course, and springs beyond the reach of his aim. Her pursuer once more gains on her; again the lariat swings through the air,—he lets go,—the noose catches her neck,—the hunter's horse turns suddenly off, and the rope, securely attached to the saddle, brings the poor captive headlong to the ground. The trained horse keeps a strain on the noose sufficient to prevent her from rising, while the hunter dismounts and secures his prize. The colts shared the same fate, and, with the mother, were subdued and made useful to the tribe.

The scenes and reminiscences I have described did not prevent the matter of most absorbing interest to myself—the projected visit to "Holland"—from engaging due attention. The chief came home from the council full of it. He was in royal good humor, and talked about it half the night; but several objections arose, which it was necessary for me to dispose of. These were met, apparently to his full satisfaction. One of the most serious was the fear that the white men would revenge upon him the murder of Captain Eaton. I assured him that so long as I was with him he had nothing to fear on that score; the people were all mine, and would do, or refrain from doing, whatever I should bid them. They would not dare to lift their hands against him contrary to my orders, or refuse to deliver what articles I chose to demand. Nothing, I found, would do, but the assertion of absolute supremacy over all white men whatever, the world around; less than this would not secure the confidence of these savages, and I regulated my speech by the necessities of the case. The chief inquired, half a dozen times over, what I would say to the white men, and I as often rehearsed an address for the occasion. At last his curiosity seemed abated, and we fell asleep.

Early the next morning we were up and stirring, and the chief having adjusted his toilet with care, a slight breakfast was made ready. This over, his highness stood forth, and from the door of his lodge made an official address to the tribe, wherein he set out the advantages of a visit to "Holland," and suggested the most expedient style of making it. He advised that a few only of the tribe should be deputed, with himself, to accompany me, and receive the stores of rum, tobacco, bread, rice, tea, butter, beads, brass, copper, and so forth, that were to be forthcoming, as the expression of my gratitude for the distinguished consideration with which they had treated me. Though royal speeches seldom excite any jealousy of plagiarism, and it may seem a little captious on my part to make such a charge, it is due to "the truth of history" to declare, that herein the great Parosilver did but repeat a suggestion which he did me the honor to receive with favor over-night. It was not deemed essential to the case to inform his highness of all the reasons that led me to wish for as small an escort as the nature of the business would admit. On the contrary, acting upon the profound maxim, that one sufficient reason is as good as a dozen, and better than that number of questionable ones, I merely advised, that, after the experience which Captain Eaton and others had had of Patagonian prowess, the sight of too many of his giants would frighten away the whites, and prevent all beneficial communication with them; while the presence of a small deputation would be a pledge of their pacific inclinations. The speech from the throne proved less moving than most of the chief's effusions: his lieges listened with great interest, and an earnest debate sprung up, at the conclusion of which it was decided that the chief, with four other Indians and their squaws, should be my body-guard, the rest of the tribe to follow after. Another old woman begged to go with us, which was agreed to. The horse I had been in the habit of riding was lame, and unfit for service; another was procured for me.

Our simple preparations for departure were soon made, and as we were about to start they all began bringing their dirty children to me, and requesting that I would bring brass and beads for them all; which was gravely promised, much to their satisfaction. There remained the last act in the comedy for which I had been long rehearsing,—if, indeed, it did not turn out a tragedy. The idea had early occurred to me, that if I had some object to which I appeared very much attached, it might prove to be for my advantage; the Indians might hold it, in my absence at any time, as a sort of surety for my return. A belle from among the beauties of the tribe would be effectual to that end; but, if no sentiments of virtue had restrained me from this expedient, the filth and unsightliness of them all were enough to insure continence. I chose, therefore, a little white dog for a pet,—a dirty, thievish little rascal;—but I fondled him in the style proper to a violent attachment. It is true that when I saw him licking the meat designed for our repast it was not easy to refrain from kicking his worthless brains out; but this was a trifle to other things I had to endure, and I made myself apparently so fond of him that the reality of the case was never suspected. Now and then I indemnified myself by giving him, when unobserved, a smart rapping for his misdeeds, though such chastisement made but a slight impression on the object of it. As we were about setting out, I was asked if I intended to take my dog. No, I told them, he would be better off there, and when I returned he should have some bread and other dainties to eat. The ruse more than answered its expected end, in lulling all suspicion of my sincerity.

At last we were under way. The grand crisis to which all my diplomacy and the utmost license of fiction had tended was near at hand. A strong hope of deliverance braced my spirits, shaded, it is true, by a natural apprehension of possible failure, and of the consequences that might follow. With no great elation of spirits, but with a stern, severe tension of all my mental energies, and a concentration of them into one focus of resolve, I waved a farewell, which I hoped might be everlasting, to the accursed gang of robbers who had tormented me so many tedious weeks. "Good-by to Patagonia!" I mentally ejaculated, and struck off with my escort; but had not gone more than an eighth of a mile, when the party wheeled about and ordered me to follow them back to the camp! I remonstrated, but it was of no use, and with a heavy heart I found myself once more in my dirty corner of a wigwam. The horses were turned adrift without a word of explanation, and the Indians sat down to a game of cards, with as much indifference to everything else as if the events of the past forty-eight hours had been a feverish dream. What could be the meaning of it? I questioned the chief. He merely replied that he would go by and by,—by and by; which, being interpreted, probably meant when he pleased, and that convenient season might never arrive! After I had teased him for a long time he took me to the door of the lodge, and, pointing to the river, said it was "no good then;" it would be "good" at night. What the state of the river, which was a shallow stream, a branch of the Santa Cruz, had to do with the matter, I could not divine, and was half inclined to vote myself fairly outwitted by the Old Boy.

The day, a long one, at last wore off, and at night we once more set off. We crossed the frozen marsh, and forded the river, and, after going about two miles, stopped for repose. We took no camp equipage, and had to shelter ourselves for the night under the lee of a clump of bushes. We thrust our feet into the thicket, while our heads lodged out of doors. In this interesting attitude I was made to repeat my wearisome detail of promises, and to rehearse once more my contemplated speech to the white men; which done, we dropped asleep. Waking early the next morning, I found my head and shoulders covered with a fleecy mantle of snow. Would the fortune of my expedition fall as lightly on me? I shook it off, turned up my coat-collar, pulled my poor, more than half worn-out cap over my ears, and so, partially protected from the storm, rolled over, and again sunk into a slumber. The storm ceased at dawn of day. I rose and went in search of fuel, while my dark companions still slept profoundly. In an hour or two they roused themselves, and kindled a fire. Meat, from a store brought along for our provision on the way, was cooked, and served for breakfast. The scanty meal being despatched, our horses were driven in, lassoed, mounted, and we resumed our journey, in a south-easterly direction. At the end of about three miles another halt was called, a fire was built to warm by, and the horses were watered. The order of arrangements was discussed, and a fresh edition of the promises and the speech critically listened to. Changing our course a little to the right, we soon struck the Santa Cruz. The Indians pointed far down the stream, and said, "There is Holland." I strained my eyes in the direction pointed out, and thought I could discern an island with several small huts upon it. A mile or two further on the north bank brought us to the mouth of the river, in prospect of the Atlantic. The island was directly opposite the mouth, and the lower part only appeared to be inhabited. We halted. The Indians pointed towards it, exclaiming, "Esta Holland sarvey! muchas casas, mucho mucho hombres, tene mucho aquadiente, mucho travac, yeruen, arenar, arose!"—This is Holland, and has plenty of houses, and abundance of men,—plenty of rum, tobacco, bread, tea, flour and rice! I surveyed the spot in silence. This island was of considerable extent, lying two-thirds across the wide mouth of the river, its surface dotted over with little knolls or hillocks of earth. Could it be that these were dwellings inhabited by white men?

Our horses' heads were now turned from the shore, and we rode back about an eighth of a mile to a large clump of bushes, unsaddled our beasts, and waited some time for the rest of our company, who had fallen in the rear. They came at last, our horses were turned adrift, fire was lighted, and, as the day was far spent, supper was in order. Then ensued a repetition—a final one, I trusted—of the grand present to be levied on the Hollanders, and of the speech which was to draw them out. The Indians arranged that I was to hoist the English flag,—the colors of the unfortunate brig Avon, which they had brought along at my request,—and then to walk the shore to attract the attention of the islanders. On the approach of a boat, I was to be kept back from the beach, to prevent escape; for I found that they were not, after all, as well assured of my good faith as might have been desirable. They thought, moreover, that when the white men saw a prisoner with them, they would come ashore to parley, and offer presents to effect his release; in that case, there might be a chance, if the negotiation proved unsatisfactory, to take bonds of fate in the form of another captive or two. So, at least there was ground to suspect,—and some cause to fear that the rascals might prove too shrewd for all of us!

After talking till a late hour, the Indians threw themselves upon the ground, stuck their feet into the bushes, and were soon fast asleep. I consulted the chief as to the propriety of modifying this arrangement, by placing our heads, rather than our feet, under cover, since both could not be accommodated. He declined any innovations, and told me to go to sleep. I stretched myself on the ground, but as to sleep, that was out of the question. I lay all night, thinking over all possible expedients for escape. We had no materials for a boat or raft of any description, and it was impossible to think of any plan that promised success; so that, after tossing, in body and mind, through the weary hours of night, I could only resolve to wait the course of events, and to take advantage of the first opportunity affording a reasonable hope of deliverance from this horrid captivity. Snow, sleet and rain, fell during the night; and I rose early, thoroughly chilled, every tooth chattering. A fire was kindled, and the last morsel of meat that remained to us was cooked and eaten. The weather continued squally till the middle of the afternoon.

After breakfast the chief went with me to the shore, bearing the flag. On the beach I found a strip of thick board, to which I fastened the colors, and then planted it in the sand. The bushes around, which have a kind of oily leaf and readily ignite, were set on fire. I then walked the beach,—but no boat came. When it cleared up sufficiently to see, I observed little objects moving about on the island. The day wore away with fruitless attempts to attract their attention. With an aching heart I returned, at dark, to the camping-ground. On this island my hopes had so long centred,—if they were now to be disappointed, how could I endure it? The Indians began to talk of rejoining the tribe the following day. I opposed the motion with all the dissuasives at command, assuring them that, at sight of our flag, the islanders would surely come over in a boat, and that, if they would only wait a little, they could go over to the island and enjoy themselves to their hearts' content; representing the absolute necessity that I should procure the rum, &c., we had talked of, and how embarrassing it would be to go back to the tribe empty-handed, after all that had been said, to be ridiculed and reproached. It would never do. Our conversation was continued till quite late, when we ranged ourselves, hungry and weary, for another night. For hours I was unable to sleep. The uncertainties of my situation oppressed me, and I lay restless, with anxiety inexpressible, inconceivable by those whom Providence has preserved from similar straits. It was a season of deep, suppressed, silent misery, in which the heart found no relief but in mute supplication to Him who was alone able to deliver. Towards morning, exhausted with the intensity of emotion acting on an enfeebled body, I slept a little, and woke at early dawn, to a fresh consciousness of my critical position.

THE ESCAPE

The weather had been fair during the night, but there were now indications of another snow-storm. I waited long and impatiently for my companions to awake, and at last started off in quest of fuel; on returning with which, they bestirred themselves and started a fire, which warmed our half-benumbed limbs. There lay the little island, beautiful to eyes that longed, like mine, for a habitation of sympathizing men, about a mile and a half distant; it almost seemed to recede while I gazed, so low had my hopes sunken, under the pressure of disappointment and bitter uncertainty. A violent snow-storm soon setting in, it was hidden from view; everything seemed to be against me. It slackened, and partially cleared up,—then came another gust, filling the air, and shutting up the prospect. In this way it continued till past noon; at intervals, as the sky lighted up, I took a fire-brand, and set fire to the bushes on the beach, and then hoisted the flag again, walking wearily to and fro, till the storm ceased, and the sky became clear. The chief concealed himself in a clump of bushes, and sat watching, with cat-like vigilance, the movements of the islanders. After some time, he said a boat was coming; I scarcely durst look in the direction indicated, lest I should experience a fresh disappointment; but I did look, and saw, to my great joy, a boat launched, with four or five men on board, and pushing off the shore. On they came; the chief reported his discovery, and the rest of the Indians came to the beach, where I was still walking backward and forward. The boat approached, not directly off where I was, but an eighth of a mile, perhaps, to the windward, and there lay on her oars.

The Indians hereupon ordered me to return to the camping-ground; but, without heeding them, I set off at a full run towards the boat. They hotly pursued, I occasionally turning and telling them to come on,—I only wanted to see the boat. "Stop! Stop!" they bawled. "Now, my legs," said I, "if ever you want to serve me, this is the time." I had one advantage over my pursuers; my shoes, though much the worse for wear, protected my feet from the sharp stones, which cut theirs at every step; but, under all disadvantages, I found they made about equal speed with myself. As I gained a point opposite the boat, the Indians slackened their speed, and looked uneasily at me; the man in the stern of the boat hailed me, inquiring what Indians these were, what number of them, and how I came among them. I replied in as few words as possible, and told him we wished to cross to the island. He shook his head; they were bad fellows, he said; he could not take me with the Indians. They began to pull away! I made signs of distress, and waved them to return, shouting to them through my hands. The boat was again backed within hailing distance. "Will you look out for me, if I come by myself?" "Yes!" was the prompt reply. The Indians, all this time, had kept within ten or fifteen feet of me, with their hands on their knives, and reiterating their commands to come back, at the same time edging towards me in a threatening manner. "Yes, yes," I told them, "in a moment," but I wanted to look at the boat,—taking care, however, to make good my distance from them. At the instant of hearing the welcome assurance that I should be cared for, I drew out the watch (which I had brought, according to promise, to have a new crystal inserted at Holland), and threw it into the bushes; the salt water would spoil it, and, if I should be retaken, the spoiling of that would be an aggravation which might prove fatal. At the same moment I gave a plunge headlong into the river; my clothes and shoes encumbered me, and the surf, agitated by a high wind, rolled in heavy seas upon the shore. The boat was forty or fifty yards off; and, as the wind did not blow square in shore, drifted, so as to increase the original distance, unless counteracted by the crew. Whether the boat was backed up towards me, I could not determine; my head was a great part of the time under water, my eyes blinded with the surf; and most strenuous exertion was necessary to live in such a sea. As I approached the boat I could see several guns, pointed, apparently, at me. Perhaps we had misunderstood each other,—perhaps they viewed me as an enemy! In fact, they were aimed to keep the Indians from following me into the water, which they did not attempt. My strength was fast failing me; the man at the helm, perceiving it, stretched out a rifle at arm's length. The muzzle dropped into the water, and arrested my feeble vision. Summoning all my remaining energy, I grasped it, and was drawn towards the boat; a sense of relief shot through and revived me, but revived, also, such a dread lest the Indians should give chase, that I begged them to pull away,—I could hold on. The man reached down, and seized me by the collar, and ordered his men to ply their oars. They had made but a few strokes, when a simultaneous cry broke from their lips, "Pull the dear man in! Pull the dear man in!" They let fall their oars, laid hold of me, and, in their effort to drag me over the side of their whale-boat, I received some injury; I requested that they would let me help myself; and, working my body up sufficiently to get one knee over the gunwale, I gave a spring, with what strength was left me, and fell into the bottom of the boat. They kindly offered to strip me, and put on dry clothes; but I told them, if they would only work the boat further from the shore, I would take care of myself. They pulled away, while I crawled forward, divested myself of my coat, and put on one belonging to one of the crew. Conversation, which was attempted, was impossible; it was one of the coldest days of a Patagonian winter,—I was chilled through, and could only articulate, "I ca-n't ta-lk now; I'll ta-lk by a-nd by." Some liquor, bread and tobacco, which had been put on board for my ransom, on supposition that this was what the signal meant, was produced for my refreshment. The sea was heavy, with a strong head-wind; so that, though the men toiled vigorously, our progress was slow. I was soon comfortably warmed by the stimulants provided, and offered to lend a hand at the oar; but the offer was declined. The shouts and screams of the Indians, which had followed me into the water, and rung hideously in my ears while struggling for life in the surf, were kept up till distance made them inaudible. Whether they found the watch, whose mysterious tick at once awed and delighted them, and restored it to its place of state in the chief's lodge, or whether it still lies rusting in the sands by the sea-shore, is a problem unsolved.

The boat at last grounded on the northern shore of the island; Mr. Hall, the gentleman who commanded the party, supported my tottering frame in landing; and, as we stepped upon the shore, welcomed me to their island. I grasped his hand, and stammered my thanks for this deliverance, and lifted a tearful eye to Heaven, in silent gratitude to God. I was then pointed to a cabin near by, where a comfortable fire was ready for me. "Now," I heard Mr. Hall say, "let us fire a salute of welcome to the stranger. Make ready! present! fire!" Off went all their muskets, and a very cordial salute it appeared to be. He soon followed me, took me to his own dwelling, supplied me with dry clothing, and, above all, warmed me in the kindly glow of as generous a heart as ever beat in human bosom.

I was captured by the savages on the 1st of May, and landed upon the island on the 7th of August.

CHAPTER IX

A civilized meal—A happy evening—A survey of the island—Preparation of guano—Preparations against invasion by the giants—A proposal to attack them—Loyalty and revenge—Killing time— Trouble in the settlement—A disagreeable situation—Arrival of vessels—Countrymen—A welcome by new friends.

After getting sufficiently thawed out, I gave a synopsis of my adventures. The cook presently laid the table, and brought in supper. I ate heartily of bread and Irish pork, and drank tea raised in Brazil, called matte. It may not compare favorably with the produce of China, but to me it was a delicious beverage. I had been in captivity ninety-seven days, living as the reader has seen. Although I partook freely of supper,—too freely for one in my weak condition,—I rose from the meal with as keen an appetite as I brought to it. I again expressed to Mr. Hall, on learning his name, my gratitude at finding myself, through his timely assistance, among friends, though a stranger. He cordially sympathized with me, observing that he had been a prisoner among the Patagonians for one day only, but had seen enough in that short time to be convinced that a life of ninety-seven days with them must have been dreadful indeed.

After supper the boat was hauled up on the island. Pipes and tobacco were furnished, and I passed in the society of my deliverers one of the happiest evenings of my whole life. The change was so great, from the miserable and almost hopeless existence I had so long lived, that my joy exceeded all bounds. My heart overflowed with gratitude. Words could not then, and cannot now, convey any adequate impression of my feelings,—of the freedom and joy that animated me, on being snatched from perils, privations and enemies, and placed, as in a moment, in security, in plenty, and in the society of friends. It seemed like a dream, the change was so sudden and so total.

The little house which for the present I called my home, and which, in fact, appeared to me at the time the pleasantest dwelling I had ever seen, was about twelve by fifteen feet upon the ground, built of boards and scantling, and lined with blue Kentucky jean. The fireplace was in the middle of one end, and a door opened at the opposite extremity. Two large closets were parted off, the one used as a cupboard, and the other for stores. Each side was lighted by a window containing four panes of seven-by-nine glass. Two comfortable settees, probably saved from some wreck, lined the sides of the room, and a good-sized hardwood table occupied the centre. It was floored overhead, and a trap-door opened into a sleeping apartment, fitted with two little berths,—one for Mr. Hall, and the other for Morrison, the Scotchman.

As we have described the interior of our snug little cottage, we will bestow a word or two on its exterior and surroundings. Its cracks and joints, over the roof and walls, were covered with strips of tarred duck, and battened with narrow pieces of thin board. It was situated on a little mound of guano, perhaps four feet high, and was banked up to the windows with the same material. The height of the walls above the embankment was about seven feet, the embankment three feet more. A ship's bell was suspended on the north-east corner of the house, to notify the workmen of the hours of labor and of their meals. Sea Lion Island, as it is called,—the name "Holland" was probably corrupted by the Indians, from the word island, indistinctly pronounced in their hearing,—is about a mile and a quarter long from north to south, with an average width of an eighth of a mile, and is covered over its entire surface with low evergreen bushes. The settlement was made by an English company, for the purpose of collecting guano and preparing it for exportation, and was situated on the southern extremity.

Our social evening was prolonged to a late hour, the moments sped by the stimulus of novel enjoyment. One of the settees was assigned for my couch, bed-clothes were provided, and a bag filled with ships' colors and other articles served for a pillow. Before committing ourselves to repose, however, we discussed the probability of an invasion from the continent, and came to the conclusion that nothing was to be feared in that quarter before morning. Old Boy and his party, it was obvious, would have to return to the main body of the tribe for reinforcements and naval equipage before attempting pursuit, as they had no materials for the construction of boats or rafts, even if they would dare to tempt salt water in their leathern sacks. We accordingly dismissed the subject for the time, and Mr. Hall and the Scotchman, having cared for my comfort with anxious kindness, disappeared through the trap-door, leaving behind a friendly benediction. The little cottage was warm; my couch was the perfection of comfort, in contrast with that which had been my lot for ninety-seven wretched nights. Above all, for the first time in so many weeks, I could lie down without the fear of treachery and violence. I was secure from savages. This indeed was luxury. I slept soundly, vying in the profundity of slumber with the immortal seven, till late in the morning. Daylight at length had dispossessed the darkness of every part of the interior, and I awoke. It was no dream. I was indeed free. Rude but unmistakable evidences of civilization surrounded me. The adventures of the preceding day flashed vividly on my hitherto clouded mind,—the suspense, the struggle, the seasonable rescue, the rejoicing welcome, the spontaneous and subduing kindnesses,—and a warm gush of tender and grateful emotion from my inmost soul thrilled and suffused my whole being. While these emotions were subsiding from the fervor of their first impulse, and the mind was gliding away into a delicious and confused revery, wherein all manner of delight seemed to encircle me as with an atmosphere, in whose genial glow all past suffering existed only for the heightening of present enjoyment, the trap-door overhead was lifted, and my generous friends dropped down with a hearty salutation. I sprang from my couch, as good as new, and younger than ever. A cheerful coal-fire was soon burning in the grate, the room was swept, breakfast was brought in and despatched, the bell rang, and the men issued forth to their daily labors, while I went out to explore my new abode.

The island is low and flat, and at high water its surface is only eight or ten feet above the water-line; but the tide here rises and falls about the same height as at the eastern mouth of the Straits of Magellan,—nearly forty-two feet. Within twenty-five feet of our house was a small store-house and shed, a hog-sty, and a large stone oven. About the same distance further on, was a house for workmen, framed of timber, and roofed and laid up at the sides with bushes; and the sides were banked and the roof coated with earth, an old sail forming the topmost and outermost feature of the edifice,—except that on one extremity of the roof a headless barrel communicated with the fireplace, and did duty very respectably as chimney and ventilator. There were no windows; the men, and whatever portion of light and air sufficed them, found ingress and egress through a door in one end. It was most evidently made for use, not for show; but appeared to be very comfortable, and was neatly fitted up with berths and benches, a table and cooking apparatus. Its occupants were eight in number,—three Frenchmen, two Spaniards, an Englishman, a Welshman and an Irishman; so that, the island having adopted (for a season, at least) a representative of the "universal Yankee nation," may be thought to have brought together samples from a pretty considerable part of mankind.

Besides these human specimens, the settlement boasted of a dog, two mature porkers, and a litter of pigs. Near the house was a large heap of guano, prepared and ready for shipping to England and the United States. The men were at work hard by digging it up. It lies on the surface of the ground to a depth of from one to three feet; is dug up and conveyed in barrows to a cleared spot, where it lies in heaps, to be sifted. Stones, feathers, sticks, and other foreign substances, are carefully removed, the larger lumps are broken up, and the cleared guano is spread out in a thin layer; when thoroughly dried, it is covered up with planks. The business was carried on by Captain Matthew S. White, an Englishman, who had then been absent for several months at Montevideo, whither he had gone to procure vessels for conveying the guano already prepared, now amounting to some fifteen hundred tons, to market. The time he fixed for his return had expired a month before my advent upon the island, and Mr. Hall was beginning to feel very anxious for him, fearing lest some accident had befallen him, and anxious for himself and his company, also, as they had but a few months' provisions; the island was rarely visited by vessels, and their only means of reaching any port, in case of extremity, were the ship's long-boat, and a whale-boat, both too small to undertake so long a voyage with any hope of safety.

The possibility that my late hospitable friends on the main land might be led, by their high consideration for me, to visit "Holland" in a body, kept us busy, during the day, in making preparations to receive them with appropriate honors. Mr. Hall, who was left in charge of the settlement during the absence of the proprietor, observed that Captain White had often expressed apprehensions that the Indians would come upon the island, some time when he was away, and murder all hands. My slipping from them in the manner I had was not an event likely to dissuade them from the attempt, or weaken their motives for making it. There were two swivels in the camp, which we mounted upon wheelbarrows, to serve as flying artillery. I ground sharp an old whaling-harpoon, and fixed a handle to it; this was slung over my couch; and a large sheath-knife, for use in case we got to close quarters, reposed under my pillow. The Indians were prowling about the shore, probably expecting to see me reäppear among them, laden with the rum and tobacco they came after, and which they had earned by boarding and lodging me so long, and by the multiplied kindnesses with which they beguiled the months of my residence among them. It is likely they think, by this time, that I have been gone a long time for it.

Before retiring for the night, we loaded our swivels to the muzzle, and fired them, to let our neighbors know that we had the wherewithal to give them a warm reception, should they see fit to make us a visit. We then reloaded the pieces, each with a dozen or more large bullets, placed them ready primed at the door, and covered the primings, to keep our powder dry. We had six or eight muskets ready loaded, enough to arm the entire garrison, with plenty of ammunition. The dog was tied to the doorhandle, to give notice of danger, and the door carefully secured. Just as we were about retiring, Bose gave a portentous bow wow! but, on going out, and taking a survey of the premises, the alarm proved to be false. All was quiet; and, with a momentary doubt of the sagacity and discretion of our sentinel, we lay down with a sense of security,—first taking the axe into the house, thinking that the cunning rogues might try to burn us out, should they find the efforts to dislodge us otherwise ineffectual. With this final precaution, our faithful sentinel chained to his post, like a Chinese soldier to his gun, we were soon sound asleep. The night passed quietly away, without any further alarm from our look-out, who was of the English pointer breed,—a sleepy, dough-faced fellow, better qualified to show the game than to occupy the responsible station to which he was promoted. He was a great coward, but that was not altogether against him; for, since the law of self-preservation applies to brutes as well as to men, fear would impel him to make some kind of demonstration on the approach of foes, if fidelity did not; and one kind of demonstration would be as useful to us as another, if only audible.

After breakfast I walked forth, and cast an anxious look through the glass to the northern shore of the main land, to see if the Indians still occupied their position, and whether they were building boats, or making any other preparations for invasion. There they were,—the patient creatures!—still posted in view of our quarters, the English flag flying on the beach. There were several dogs on the shore, and among them I recognized my own; I almost fancied I could hear him barking. As we brought no dogs with us, I concluded that they had gone back to the main body, and got a reinforcement, with materials for boat-building, and brought my dog for the especial gratification of his affectionate master; and now he was capering about on the shore, as if to call me back. Having sufficiently gratified my curiosity in this direction, I turned the glass seaward, in hope to view some approaching sail but the broad expanse was clear,—no vessel to be seen. On the river banks a few stray guanacos were cropping the scanty, rank grass, while others, with their young, were lying on the sunny slopes of the sand-hills. The quiet of these animals assured me that their inveterate enemies, the Indians, were not in the vicinity.

Tired, at length, of this sort of sight-seeing, I returned to the house, and, taking our guns, started with Mr. Hall on a stroll up the island, hoping to shoot some sea-fowl; but returned at noon, unsuccessful. The afternoon was spent in wandering aimlessly over the island, killing time. Walking about on the sea-shore, I picked up some clear, transparent stones, coated on the outside with a kind of crust; some of them are very hard, and, when broken, cut glass like a diamond. I wrote my name, and place of residence, on a window of our little cottage, with a fragment of one; they are mostly white, some of them of a vermilion, and others of a straw color; they are, I suppose, a variety of quartz. The shore is, in some places, covered with these pebbles to the depth of two or three feet, on an average of the size of a walnut; the hardest specimens were not abundant, but I collected about a hundred of them. I might have picked up many more, if they had possessed any special value.

A further examination of the opposite shore disclosed Indians still prowling about, and I proposed to Mr. Hall to go over, with the men, and give them a sound drubbing. Revenge, I know, is said to dwell in little minds; if so, my abode in Patagonia must have dwarfed and contracted my own intellect for the time being, for I must confess to the consciousness of a desire to visit upon them some appropriate return for what they had inflicted upon me. Mr. Hall admitted the ill-desert of the Indians, and the entire rightfulness of a severe chastisement; but, not having the same stimulus to heat his blood that burned within me, he viewed the question with a more strict regard to prudence, and was altogether disinclined to undertake so hazardous an expedition; he dreaded going any nearer to the savages than was necessary. I would, myself, rather have been shot than fall into their hands a second time; but contended that the approach of the boat would bring them to the shore, and enable us to do them a mischief from the boat, without any necessity of landing among them. True, the Indians might succeed in getting upon the island some night, and effect our destruction; there certainly was nothing to prevent it, if they had the least ingenuity, and a moderate share of courage; but I knew them to be a gang of arrant cowards, and the reader may judge of their inventiveness by the preceding narrative. The subject was discussed till late in the evening, and the needful preparations and precautions were thoroughly talked over. When about to retire for the night, we went out and looked for our vigilant sentinel, whose due place, in right of his office, should have been at the door. Recreant to his trust, the rascal had deserted, to take up his night's lodging with the pigs. He was soon hustled out of his nest, and compelled to return to the door, there to be tied, as on the preceding night, to the handle. His choice of such mean company greatly lowered the animal in my estimation. While fixing him in his place, we perceived a light on the north shore; it appeared to be carried about from place to place, and was at some distance from the Indians' wigwams. This had much the appearance of preparation for a nocturnal visit from the rascals,—a symptom of boat-building. From my observation of their habits while among them, I was convinced that something extraordinary was on foot; they were not much in the habit of moving about after dark, with or without lights, and nothing but the pressure of an unaccustomed purpose could have made them so enterprising now. We uncovered the priming of our swivels, and greased their muzzles, to make them speak in a louder tone of warning and defiance to the enemy; they were discharged with a loud report, that made the island ring, and must have resounded with effect upon the hostile shore. The guns were reloaded, primed, and mounted upon their carriages at the door. The lights that had drawn forth this sonorous demonstration speedily disappeared; the Indians, it was presumed, had taken the hint, and abandoned or postponed their undertaking, whatever it might have been. I well knew their dread of big guns. When I attempted, at first, to persuade them to go with me to Port Famine, the chief reason assigned, besides the superior advantages of "Holland," was, that there were big guns there, which were "no good for Indians." A council of war came to the conclusion that there was nothing to be feared from them that night, and we thereupon retired.

If our careful preparations seem to belie my expressed belief of their cowardice, it should be remembered that they had once fleshed their swords, if not their teeth, in the bodies of some white men, and had held, for a brief period, islanders in their custody; they were numerous, and might so far confide in their numbers and strength as to dare the attempt to wreak their disappointments fully upon our heads. Our caution was reasonable, and, at the time, was not excessive in degree. In the morning we made a careful survey of the premises, exploring all the sheds, and every other place where an enemy could have secreted himself, but made no discoveries. We walked over the island, and examined the opposite shore; but perceived nothing strange or alarming, except that the Indians still remained in their quarters, and that their numbers had greatly increased.

The question of crossing over and driving them off was revived after breakfast, but, after considerable talk, no definite conclusion was reached, and I spent the day wandering over the island, gunning and picking up rare stones, occasionally surveying the coast through the glass. At night no lights appeared opposite; and having made our usual preparations against a nocturnal attack, we decided that if the black rascals did not speedily pick up their traps, and make themselves "scarce," we would go over and hurry their movements. Mr. Hall found his loyalty stirring within him, in aid of revenge. He said it was too much to see that blood-stained British flag flying among such a miserable set of creatures, bringing freshly before his mind the forms of his slaughtered countrymen. This sentiment I was prompt to encore, and to enforce the propriety of an invasion to wrest the trophy from their hands. This was determined upon for the next day, unless they should sooner relieve us of their presence.

The day dawned with a cloudy sky and a thick atmosphere, which made it impossible to see distinctly for any distance. Towards noon it cleared up, and we discovered that our troublesome neighbors were still there. We thereupon set about the necessary preparations for a movement, immediately after dinner. Arms and equipments were appointed, knives sharpened, guns put in order and stacked against the house;—the bell rang for dinner, and we ate with appetites sharpened by excitement. But, on going out, and taking a final look through the glass before embarking, we observed the Indians catching their horses. They speedily mounted their beasts, and rode off. Our anticipated valor was soon cooled. They had slipped away without giving us a chance to do anything for revenge, for justice, or for the honor of the captive flag. On the whole, we were not sorry to abandon the expedition, though it seemed to me that our chances of security were not much improved by their departure. They would be very likely to lurk in the vicinity, and to return with full preparations for crossing and landing upon the island. Perhaps their movement was only a ruse to put us off our guard. Such thoughts crowded my mind; but there was no use in borrowing trouble, and I dismissed them.

The men returned to their work, and I set myself to devise some employment. I had become tired of idleness, and offered to assist in the preparation of guano; but Mr. Hall interposed a decided veto. He wished me, he said, to make myself entirely contented, and as comfortable as possible. But the sort of life I was leading was very decidedly uncomfortable; and I entreated so earnestly to be allowed to make myself useful in some way, that he set me to make a row-lock for a boat, or a few thole-pins, or some other trivial things, that served to occupy attention and divert the mind. Then our cottage wanted a new floor, and some alterations were found necessary about the premises. When everything was done, and no more was suggested, I was desired to go a gunning, to vary the supplies for the table, or to take a basket and pick the tops of the bushes for pickling. The bushes, which are evergreen, have on their tops little clusters not unlike barberries, that make a very fine pickle. Several jars were filled, and furnished an excellent condiment for our suppers.

Time passed on, and the non-arrival of Captain White made it drag slowly. I had thought to take passage in one of the guano vessels to Rio Janeiro, or some other South American port, from which it might be easy to obtain a passage for California. In default of other occupation, the large lighter, which lay up the creek, two-thirds the length of the island, was brought down opposite the house for repair, to be in readiness to load the ships when they should arrive. Their delay threatened us with famine, moreover, and it was beginning to be felt as a very serious matter. To add to our troubles, the scurvy broke out among the men, in consequence of living on salt provisions, without vegetables. They had been recommended, as a preventive, to make and eat freely of the pickle just described; but, either from want of faith in the virtue of the prescription, or because it was too much trouble, they had neglected to do so, and now found themselves in a poor plight.

About the same time, as troubles

"—come not single spies,
But in battalions,"

Mr. Hall was informed by the Welshman, who appeared very friendly, that Morrison, the Scotchman, was trying to prejudice the Frenchmen and Spaniards against him, and inciting the men to mutiny. The man had lived in the house and been treated like a gentleman, and this was all the return he made for the preference shown him. Sawney's goods and chattels were forthwith thrown out of doors, and he was ordered to take his bed and board with the men. He took this descent in the world very much to heart, and when I talked with him on the impropriety of his conduct, appeared quite penitent. I strongly advised Mr. Hall to take him back into the house; for, though he had proved treacherous, it was better, after all, to have him under our immediate watch than with the men, as he might, in a short time, infect the whole company. After much coaxing, consent was given to his return, and he replaced his things in the house with much apparent gratitude. He was told that he must show himself an honest man, and labor to undo the mischief he had done, if he had any care of his personal safety; for should any trouble break out, and the sacrifice of life become necessary, his would be the first. He faithfully promised, and, I doubt not, exerted himself to allay discontents and prevent any outbreak. With the Spaniards he was successful; but the Frenchmen were more turbulent, and determined on a rupture. They complained that their allowance of food was insufficient, and threatened to break into the store-house and help themselves. Mr. Hall had served out their daily rations of meat, bread and flour, by weight, according to the directions of Captain White. The quantity I have forgotten, but remember Mr. Hall saying that it was the same as is allowed per man in the British navy. When the bell rang for work the next morning, the Welshman and Irishman alone went. The Spaniards said that they had the scurvy so badly they were unable to work; the Frenchmen marched up to the house, and peremptorily demanded more flour. Mr. Hall met them at the door; and, in reply, told them that they had the same food, in quality and quantity, with all the others, himself included, and that the allowance for the house proved to be more than we needed. None of the other men complained, and their complaints could not be listened to by him. They had all that Captain White allowed, and, if they were not satisfied, they could appeal to him when he returned, which would undoubtedly be very soon. Meanwhile he advised them "to be quiet, and do their own business." They left in a very wrathful mood, not to their work, but to their quarters, and to idle away the rest of the day in sauntering up and down the island. They went on in this way for nearly a week, and at last consented to return to duty, under a promise that nothing should be deducted from their wages, which was given as a matter of prudence. It was not thought safe, in present circumstances, to strain authority over them. Nothing occurred to give serious uneasiness, though the men were so touchy and quarrelsome as to raise a slight tempest, now and then. On one occasion, Mr. Hall had been with three men up the creek, seven or eight miles, after fresh water, which could only be obtained at that distance and boated down to the settlement. While we were unlading the boat, a row was kicked up between one of the Frenchmen and the Welshman. Taffy, who was a thorough seaman, when adjusting the ropes to the casks, was assailed by one of the Frenchmen with some derogatory remark touching his seamanship, prompted by his mode of "putting on the parbuckle." The critic attempted to take the rope into his own hands, by way of enforcing and exemplifying his view of the process; and the two were on the point of settling the question in a summary fashion, in a spirit which it required some effort to quell.

The Indians still hovered in the vicinity of the further shore, as the smoke of their fires plainly indicated, and we were obliged to keep up our preparations for defence. There was nothing to prevent them from paying us a visit but their cowardice; and knowing their revengeful tempers, and the tenacity of their purposes,—the long-lived malice with which they were capable of pursuing any evil designs,—it seemed not unlikely that, smarting under the disappointment I had caused them, their resentment would prove strong enough to overcome their timidity. In this connection I had an unpleasant thought, now and then, of a hint given them while we were on our way to "Holland." When about a mile distant from the shore, I picked up a bit of plank, and somewhat rashly, in the impetuosity of desire to contrive ways and means to get to the island, in case the islanders could not be attracted towards us, told the Indians that, if we could find two or three more of the same sort, I could bind them together and make a raft, on which I might be paddled over to "Holland." I informed them, moreover, what was the most favorable time for crossing; namely, at the last of the tide, as the distance to be passed would be less, and there would be no difficulty in effecting a landing on the island. No additional materials presented themselves, and the scheme was given up; happily there was no need of it. But, less happily, it now occurred to me that what I then spoke in my own behoof might be turned by the Indians to theirs, to our no small danger, in case a more earnest and vigorous search should disclose, along-shore, more abundant materials for extemporizing transport craft.

Some of the men became so sorely afflicted with the scurvy that we decided to land on the south shore and chase some of the guanaco for fresh provision. Two of the Frenchmen accompanied us. Just as we were getting off, their countryman who was left behind came running to us, with angry jabber and gesture, vociferating that one of them had his gun. He seized it and was taking it out of the boat, when the party dispossessed of it disputed his progress, and a regular French fight of kicking and fisticuffs ensued, which we had difficulty in subduing. At last we got off, but discovered only a lone guanaco in a hollow between the hills. We posted ourselves to surround him for a shot. When he came out I had a fine chance at him as he crossed the top of the hill, and made quite sure of him. Unluckily, the flint-lock missed fire, and, before it was possible to burn any powder, our expected prey escaped. We cruised about for several miles, and returned home tired and empty.

The men continued their work, as usual, the next day; but a storm was brewing. On the following morning the Frenchmen marched up to the house, and demanded their wages. They were told by Mr. Hall that he had none of the proprietor's money, nor any authority to settle with them. Then they would work no longer. Very well, they were told, they might let work alone, but their wages and rations could not be meddled with on demand. So they indulged in another season of idleness and mischief. Their first revenge was taken on old "John," the horse. On the second day of their mutiny the poor animal was seen to halt; a hamstring was cut. He was very fat, and was probably marked by them for food, in default of fresh provision. At all events, Mr. Hall ordered him, as he was useless, to be so dealt with. The men's rations were served out, and the rest was laid up in the store-house for future use. "Horse-beef" has a strong and singular flavor. I had become accustomed to such diet among the Patagonians, though never privileged to partake of so fat a specimen as old John.

Not knowing to what height the mutinous spirit of his men might carry them, Mr. Hall wrote a brief statement of his affairs, and an account of my arrival on the island, and enclosed them, together with what money and valuable papers he had, in a tin box, which he buried at night in a guano-heap. That would certainly be removed on Capt. White's arrival, or by some one else, if he never returned; so that our tale would not be lost, even though we should not survive to tell it. The desperate character of the men,—all but one or two of whom, as we had reason to believe, had left their country for their country's good,—and the recklessness of their behavior, made our situation rather ticklish. Our fear of the Indians, moreover, was not laid entirely to sleep, though all visible tokens of their neighborhood to us had disappeared. By passing up and crossing the river, they might approach us from the south shore, which was separated from the island by a channel not more than half as broad as that on the opposite side. The bank, to be sure, was steep and muddy, involving the risk that they would be hopelessly bemired in attempting to land; but this was a weak security against them, if they were resolute enough to make the effort. Nothing occurred for several days to break the monotony of life. No work was done; the men received their allowances twice a week, spending their time in wandering over the island. The large boat needed repairs, but they rendered no aid. We took advantage of high water, rove tackles, and, by the help of rollers, drew it up high and dry on the land. When it was finished,—through fear that the men might seize it and make off to some place northward, thus depriving us of our only means of escape, if our provisions should be exhausted before Capt. White's return,—it was turned over, and the sails and oars were secured, as far as possible, from depredation.

Old John was devoured, to the partial relief of the company; but some were still badly affected with scurvy. Yet we were afraid to go any distance in search of fresh provisions, on account of the risk of finding Indians about. The carcass of a guanaco, just killed by the dogs, was picked up in time to afford a sensible alleviation of suffering, and to replenish our rapidly wasting stock of provisions. Indians without, discontent and mutiny within, and the possibility of famine, together, would have made the island anything but a paradise to one who had not so lately escaped the purgatorial pains of a Patagonian captivity. The first of these disagreeables, however, began to be less vividly felt. We got tired of sweeping the horizon with our glass in search of the smoke of their camp-fires, or other appearances suggesting their vicinity, and gradually relaxed our vigilance. Bose was released from his sentry duties, and suffered to exchange such unwilling service for the society of his friends the pigs. But we still took the axe into the house by night, and kept our guns loaded. The boat had to be launched once more, to go up the creek for water. When it was unladed, we got the aid of a Spaniard and Frenchman in drawing it on land, to prevent the rascals from stealing it, by telling them that it needed painting, which was true enough. The seine was next got out, to see if some fish could not be had for the improvement of our diet; but we got what is vulgarly termed "fisherman's luck," and spread the ineffectual net on the gravelly beach to dry. Grown desperate, at last, we decided that, Indians or no Indians, we must have fresh provisions, if any were to be had, and manned the whale-boat for an expedition to the continent. We landed on the south shore, and succeeded in discovering and bringing down a solitary guanaco. The game was dressed, and we returned to our home in triumph. The two following days were chiefly spent in hunting, unsuccessfully.

In the afternoon of the second day, having nothing else to pass away the hours, I commenced repairing the lighter, but had not been long at work before Mr. Hall came down, with a smile. "Look out to sea!" he exclaimed; "Captain White is coming." I looked as directed, and saw distinctly two sail approaching. A thrill of joy shot through me; I thought no more of work that day. An examination through the glass made them out to be a ship and a fore-and-aft schooner. Could it be any one else than Captain White? The island was not frequented by vessels except for guano; but it seemed very strange to see a schooner, as a vessel of that rig was not adapted to such a service. Mr. Hall began to think it might be some of General Rosas' vessels despatched to drive away people engaged in taking guano on the Patagonian coast. It had been reported, some time before, that he designed doing so. He heard the rumor a few months previous at Montevideo; and also another, that the Chilian government claimed the country, and were determined to hold it.

The little schooner led the way, considerably in advance of the ship. As the vessels approached nearer, they presented a decidedly Yankee look. We watched them with intense interest, as they passed the shoals, and came up with a favorable breeze, under a press of sail. Soon they entered the river's mouth. On passing the north point the schooner stood up, keeping the north shore, and cast anchor. It was evident they were not acquainted with the navigation, as there is a large shoal running from the upper end of the island nearly to the mouth of the river, and they had sailed within it. On discovering the error, she attempted to keep off, but, in so doing, struck the lower end of the shoal. Mr. Hall manned the boat, and boarded the schooner. She proved to be the Washington, tender to the ship Hudson, Captain Clift, of Mystic, Connecticut,—a whaling vessel, just from the Falkland Islands. Mr. Hall promised to go on board again during the following forenoon, and pilot the vessel into the channel.

I went with him for this purpose; and, as it was calm, the anchor was hove aweigh, and, with the boat ahead, we towed the schooner across the shoal, which at low water is plainly to be seen, but now, at flood tide, had plenty of water. After getting into the right position, the anchor was dropped, and we spent the day on board very pleasantly. The weather held moderate till afternoon. The ship yet lay off the mouth of the harbor, and made slow progress upward. The schooner, the day before, being so far ahead, had only daylight and wind enough to get in; and the ship, finding she would be benighted, as the wind sank with the sun, hauled on and off during the night, and then lay with scarcely wind enough to fill the sails. A smart breeze, however, sprung up in the afternoon, and she came gallantly into port, only repeating the mistake made by the schooner between the channels; but got off at night with the tide, and, after some delay, anchored securely in sufficient depth of water. As she intended making some stay in port, she was subsequently taken further up to the proper anchorage, and was moored on the 5th of October, having come in on the 4th.

Captain Clift had been informed by the mate, who had been ashore, and by Mr. Hall, of my misfortunes and adventures among the Patagonians, and on the following day sent a message inviting me on board his vessel. He received me very cordially, and insisted that I should make his ship my home as long as it should suit my convenience to do so. I accepted his kind offer, first going on shore, and communicating it to my liberal benefactor, Mr. Hall. He at once assented that it would undoubtedly be pleasanter to be with my countrymen. I could not leave him, however, without endeavoring to express my earnest gratitude for my rescue from a captivity worse almost than death, and for the kindly sympathy and generous hospitality that he had exercised for two months. In my destitute condition I had nothing but thanks to give, and I fervently hoped he might never be in a situation to need the like kindness from others; but he was assured, that whenever or however it might be possible to show my gratitude in a more substantial manner, it would be my happiness to do so. He begged me to give myself no trouble on that score, insisted on my retaining the articles of clothing with which he had supplied me, hoped I would come often and see him while the vessels continued there, and I bade this noble specimen of the true-hearted Englishman a tearful good-by.

CHAPTER X

A Christian ship-master—Cruise for whales, and for a California-bound vessel—An outlandish craft— An American vessel—Passage secured for California—Tempestuous passage through the Straits of Magellan—Warlike demonstrations, with an inglorious issue—Chilian penal settlement—Pleasing reception—Extensive coal-mine—Sea-lions—Mutiny of the convicts, and awful fate of the governor and chaplain.

Captain Clift cordially welcomed me to his ship, and immediately tendered me whatever I might need for personal comfort. I declined availing myself of his generosity, assuring him that I could be comfortable with present supplies; but he insisted on replenishing my wardrobe, silencing all objections by the remark that I plainly needed the articles, and that it was a part of our duty on earth to give to the needy. Captain Clift was a Christian in precept and example. He had daily prayer on board his ship, and made his religion an inseparable part of himself; something more than a profession, that did not expend itself in words, but found expression in acts of kindness to all within his reach. He had on board a poor sick Irish lad, who was taken into the cabin, and nursed with all the care that circumstances admitted. Had poor Mike been his own son, he could not have done more for him. Such acts, incapable of being traced to any sordid or selfish motive, sprung spontaneously from his capacious heart, full to overflowing with the milk of human kindness. As the ship had been at the Falkland Islands for several months, where they lived exclusively upon fresh meat, it seemed impossible that there should be a case of scurvy on board; but the captain remarked that the Patagonian coast was the worst he ever visited in this respect.

The crew, under direction of the mate, a brother of the captain, were busy in landing cattle, swine, empty casks and other articles, to make room on board for trying out whales, in case they captured any more, for which the schooner was getting ready to cruise up and down the coast. The mate went in the tender on her first trip out; but she returned, in three or four days, unsuccessful. A second cruise was undertaken, but in a week's absence only one whale was discovered, and this they failed to secure. A third and still longer trip was equally unsuccessful, and they returned not a little discouraged. During this time I had repeatedly exchanged visits with Mr. Hall, and felt quite comfortable in my new quarters; but suffered the misery of idleness, and of impatience at my detention, even among such generous and considerate friends. Partially to relieve the tedium of inactivity, in compliance with an urgent request for some useful employment, I was allowed to repair the ship's spanker. But I determined that, on the next cruise of the tender, I would take a berth, in the hope of falling in with some vessel bound around Cape Horn, or to Montevideo, Rio Janeiro, Pernambuco, or any other port from which it might be possible to secure a passage to California,—a land I was resolved at least to see, after having got so far on my way, though so inauspiciously.

The vessel was soon ready to sail. The evening before our departure Mr. Hall visited me, and also came in the morning, before we were off;—the whole-souled fellow! I shall always pray for his happiness. Captain Clift added to his other kindnesses by pressing upon me various articles of comfort for the voyage, with a nice clothes-bag to contain them all. I parted from them, heartily praying a continuance of God's blessing on them both; adding, however, that it was very likely they would see me turning up among them, like a bad penny, on the return of the schooner. In truth, my natural buoyancy had so far died out, that but faint hopes of a successful termination of the voyage, begun, so long before, under auspices apparently cheering, now encouraged me. We hove up the anchor, hoisted sail, and steered out of the harbor and down the coast, running off and standing in on the land, in hope to fall in with whales. On the fourth day out, we discovered a sail coming down the coast towards us. It proved to be an outlandish-looking craft, from her rig appearing to be a Portuguese schooner. We sailed towards her with a light breeze, lowered our boat, and went alongside the foreigner. She had on board a large crew of cut-throat looking fellows, loitering about. We were not asked on board, but remained in the boat talking with them through one of our men, a Portuguese. They said they were from some place, the name of which I have now quite forgotten, up the Straits of Gibraltar, and were bound through the Straits of Magellan to California. I suggested to Mr. Clift the propriety of getting on board, and going to Port Famine or to California. He said I could do as I pleased; but that, for his own part, he would feel hardly willing to trust himself among them, in which opinion I concurred.

Our Portuguese hand went on board, and talked with the captain of my adventures among the Indians, and of the occupation, &c., of our schooner. He was directed to inquire for whales, and brought us answer that several had been seen along the coast, some distance to the northward. While this conversation was going on, a tall, hairy fellow came up from the cabin, encased in a dark-colored cloak having a red collar, and stripes of the same hue running about the edge; a hood, or cap, of divers gaudy colors, lay back on his shoulders, and another, gayly and profusely variegated in hue, was perched upon his head. Altogether he was a comical-looking piece of human nature. He took a look at our vessel through the glass. In answer to an inquiry through our interpreter, we learned that they had passed, the day before, an American schooner bound that way, which could not be far off. One of the sailors passed some liquor to us over the side of the vessel; it was sad stuff, and I could only out of compliment go through with the form of drinking. While this little courtesy was enacting, our Esau over-head was scanning the horizon with his glass, and at length exclaimed that he saw the vessel; we turned, and distinctly perceived a sail making towards us.

We soon returned to the tender, and stood in for the shore, in order to cut off the approaching stranger; anxious to meet her, I went aloft to the mast-head, where the view was better, and kept the mate advised of her course. When near enough to be watched from the deck, I came down, as it was impossible she could escape us. Mr. Clift offered to board her, and I accordingly picked up my things, ready for contingencies; the breeze was light, and the strange schooner approached slowly. We stood in till it was judged we were in her track, and then hove to, with the stars and stripes flying at the main gaff, as a signal that we wished to speak her. Presently the same beautiful flag was run up her main peak; on she came,—our boat was lowered, Mr. Clift jumped in with me, and we were rowed alongside, the schooner rounding to, and laying by for us to come on board. Captain Clift announced himself to the master of the schooner, who came to the side to receive us, and introduced me. He courteously invited us on board, jocosely remarking that we had a good many captains for one vessel, took us into the cabin, and treated us with the greatest civility.

The schooner proved to be the Hopewell, of New Orleans, Captain Morton, from Antigua, and bound to San Francisco, through the Straits of Magellan. There were two passengers aboard, an American gentleman, and a Portuguese, taken aboard at Bahia. At Captain Morton's request, I gave a sketch of my expedition and sojourn among the cannibals. "You were bound to California when you embarked?" he inquired, when I had concluded; "I am bound there, and, if you wish to finish your voyage, you can go with me." My mind was relieved; I almost feared to ask a passage, but my wish had been anticipated,— my request generously granted before it was uttered. I gratefully accepted his offer; remarking that unless my vessel had arrived in safety, of which I had no assurance, I should find myself as destitute on landing as at that moment; but that he could leave me at Port Famine, if I became troublesome. The "John Allyne" I supposed to have been lost soon after my capture; I had heard nothing of her since. He desired me to give myself no trouble in that matter on his account, and exerted himself to entertain us. As we were opposite the river Gallegos, and could easily run down to Cape Virgin during the night, Captain Morton felt in no hurry; and the whaling schooner was very well posted for observation on the coast, so that our men were well contented, and we had a very pleasant social interview of two or three hours. Finally, after partaking of some refreshments, I bade adieu to my excellent friend Mr. Clift, and the two vessels parted, to pursue their different courses.

During the night, we worked our way down to the straits. I sat up quite late with the captain; and, when at length I retired to my state-room, fell soundly asleep. The next morning we were nearly opposite Cape Virgin, the north point of the entrance to the straits. We were rather wide off the cape; the wind was ahead, and a good strong breeze; we beat in at last, and anchored under Point Dungeness. The Portuguese schooner was in the offing; she worked up before night, and anchored a little to the windward of us. We lay at anchor through the night; the next morning we both got under way, with a light breeze, which lasted, however, but a little while, when the wind came round ahead. As we were passing Point Dungeness,—it was not fairly daylight, and I had not yet risen,—Mr. F., one of the passengers, cried out that the shore opposite was lined with Indians. I hurried on deck, to get a peep at them; upon looking, there appeared a great school of seals on the beach; they seemed to be standing up, and walking on their hind feet, so as to have, in the dusk, very much the appearance of Indians. With some difficulty we worked up to near the point where the John Allyne lay when I made my unlucky visit on shore, and came to anchor; so that I was brought back again almost to the starting-point of this "eventful history,"—a revolution suggestive of many reflections.

The next day there came a heavy gale; the Portuguese schooner had anchored on the preceding night, in the bight of Possession Bay, further down. We lay heavily pitching at our anchors till afternoon, when Captain Morton determined to get his anchors, if possible, and run down to where the foreign schooner lay, thinking it might prove a safe anchorage. After much trouble in raising the anchors, we ran back, keeping the lead going, and running at a furious rate, under bare poles, excepting the head of the jib. The whole bay was a sheet of surf and foam. I began to think we had not much bettered our condition by removing. We anchored abreast of our Portuguese friend, but still dragged the anchors. We finally brought up by securing some iron castings we had on board to the kedge; the chain-cable was reeved through them,—they were let down ten or fifteen feet from the anchor. The small kedge thus fixed, with the weight attached to the chain, ploughed to the bottom, instead of being lifted out by the strain on the cable, thereby performing the service of one many times its weight. Our little vessel rode out the gale, which was of short duration; as the sun went down the wind subsided. We had hoisted a small sail to the main-mast, in shape resembling a leg of mutton, to make the vessel ride head to the wind, instead of lying in the trough of the sea. The tide, running at the time strongly against the wind, caused us to lie nearly broadside to the force of the gale; but this temporary sail, supplying the place of after-sail, caused the craft to lie more steadily. Just before sunset we got our anchors at the bow, and were under close-reefed sail, beating back to the place we left in the forenoon, near the first narrows. We arrived there in the evening, and again anchored; the next morning, with a light breeze from the eastward, we stood into the narrows, in company with the Portuguese schooner. Soon after we had passed through the narrows, the wind came ahead; we beat along, and anchored under Cape Gregory, a fine anchorage.

Towards evening we discovered something sitting upon a high, abrupt sand-cliff, on the bordering shore; we could perceive, by an occasional movement, that it was a living creature. The object was of considerable interest, and was closely inspected with the glass; at last it was pronounced to be an Indian. The shore was closely scanned in all directions, to ascertain whether there were more in the vicinity; none were in sight, and we concluded to pay the solitary a visit; but, as hundreds might be concealed in the neighborhood, we armed to the teeth. Old flint-lock muskets, rusty with long idleness, were dragged from their hiding-places, and treated to a dose of oil, to limber their aged joints; new flints were fitted to the locks, and everything put in good order. The guns were heavily charged with powder and shot; pistols and cutlasses, dirks and bowie-knives, were all in readiness, and the boat was alongside, manned by the sailors ready to receive us. Mr. F., the first and second mates, and myself, pushed off for the shore. We landed at some distance from the object of our visit, that we might have a better opportunity to survey the country around. Before the boat fairly felt the bottom, the second mate jumped into the water, and ran along the beach, until he could see that the supposed Indian was a large bird. He raised his gun, and fired; the bird came tumbling down the precipice, and, on running up, we found it to be a large condor. The Dutchman had broken his wing. We caught our prize and took it on board the vessel, and were heartily laughed at for our pains by the captain, who had been viewing the onslaught through the glass. Mr. F. was teased by him many days for the intrepidity of his charge on the poor bird, rushing to the attack with a drawn sword in one hand, and a cocked pistol in the other. We all felt a little crest-fallen, I must admit, after having made such formidable preparations for an Indian fight, to return with so inglorious a prize; but, as none of my former tormentors could reasonably be supposed to have strayed to this part of the country, and I had no animosities towards other tribes to be gratified, I felt, on the whole, very well satisfied with the result. We measured the bird; but, as I was not "takin' notes" at the time, it is now impossible to give its dimensions; it was very large.

The next day we commenced beating under a head-wind through the second narrows; but, when partially through, it commenced blowing so severely that we were compelled to return to our anchorage at Cape Gregory. The following day we double-reefed the sails, beat through the narrows, and anchored in Oazy Harbor. Here we went on shore, and discovered traces of Indians; the smoke of their fires was seen to the westward. We roamed about on shore for some hours, but found nothing to interest us; it was all exceeding bare and monotonous. The breeze continuing fresh ahead, we remained one day in the harbor, spending our leisure in shooting sea-fowls, which were very abundant. Once more we got under way, and anchored off the mouth of Pecket Harbor until daylight, then stood into Royal Road, and passed to the westward of Elizabeth Island into Catalina Bay.

Before passing Sandy Point, we saw several horses, and a Chilian flag flying. We hauled in and came to anchor, as we wished to procure wood and water. A large gathering of Spaniards from the settlement came to the shore. Among them I noticed a little man, handsomely dressed, with a beautiful cloak, and a cap having a wide gilt band; he appeared to be about fifty years old. A young man, of perhaps thirty, of fine appearance, accompanied him. He was dressed in military costume, blue trousers with white side-stripe, blue coat with standing collar, and cloth cap with a gilt band. These important personages were no less than the governor and his highest officer. They were walking along in conversation, and came down to meet us as we landed, shaking hands, and asking us where we were from, whither bound, and if we stood in need of anything. Capt. Morton could understand the Spanish, when spoken, easier than he could speak it himself. I therefore acted as spokesman, and replied that we wanted wood and water. After learning the quantity needed, his excellency gave his men orders to cut and split the wood, and draw it to the shore; and said that if we would send our water-casks ashore, his men should fill them. In due time both orders were executed, and we received a good supply of these necessary stores. We were then invited to the governor's house. His table was sumptuously spread, and we were entertained in the most handsome style. He was a kind, gentlemanly man, and refused to receive a penny for the supplies he furnished us, but accepted some presents from the captain. The young officer also treated us very politely, and hospitably entertained us in his house. Our vessel remained here about a week. Every day the governor sent us a large bucket of sweet milk, and sometimes fresh beef. The place was a Chilian penal settlement. He was about removing the colony from Port Famine here, on account of the superiority of the soil. The young soldier and the Catholic padre were his principal officers. A part of the colony yet remained at Port Famine.

One day, while walking out with the governor to look at the settlement, he asked if we were acquainted with coal. I replied, pointing to Mr. F., that he had been an engineer on several steamboats, and ought to be able to judge of carbon, as they called it. He sent his men along the little brook to look for some. They soon returned with several small specimens, which Mr. F. pronounced good coal. The governor said that the little brook led up to a large coal-mine, six or seven miles back, and he requested us to go and look at it. The next day he renewed the proposal, offered us horses and a man to clear the way, and said the padre would accompany us. I hesitated a little, suggesting that we might fall in with Indians. But he said, and the priest concurred, that there was no danger on that score, and we consented to go. We accordingly went on shore the following morning, and found horses in readiness for us. Mr. F., the padre and myself, started off, accompanied by a Spaniard on foot, armed with an axe, to clear away the obstructions in our path. After leaving the settlement, we plunged into a thick wood, on low, marshy ground, and followed a blind trail, leading now over the trunk of a large tree, which our horses leaped with difficulty, now across a quagmire, which had to be filled with bushes to furnish a foothold, and again was obstructed by an overhanging tree, or pendent branch, which arrested our progress till it could be cut away. In this manner we worked a passage for about a mile, when we emerged into an upland region free from underbrush. By this time, the thought recurred that it was rather imprudent travelling unarmed in that miserable country, infested by savage men and wild beasts; but I was in for it, and jogged along with dogged resolution. The face of the country became more uneven as we proceeded, tall trees were numerous, and we caught an occasional glimpse of snow on the hills. We soon reached a height at which there was abundance of snow. Our guide strode in advance, his Spanish axe swung upon his shoulder, calmly whistling a tune to himself. As we were descending a steep place, my horse suddenly stopped, and bent his head and legs to the ground,—the saddle slipped over his head, and his rider instantly found himself about thirty feet below, his head and hands stuck fast in the snow, and his heels elevated high in air. A little smart exertion extricated me from my uncomfortable position. Our guide came to me, uttering maledictions on the stumbling beast. Clambering with me back to where the horse stood, he beat him soundly, and again girt the saddle so tightly that I almost feared it would sever his body. I remonstrated, but he replied that it was a bad horse, and was playing old tricks. At the bottom of the declivity I remounted; we travelled through the snow as far as we could ride, then left our horses and continued our way on foot. The snow was very deep, in places frozen hard enough to bear our weight. A walk of a mile or more brought us, with some fatigue, to the coal-mine. But there was such a depth of snow that we could see only here and there a projection of coal in the banks of the brook which runs down from the mountains to the settlement.

The coal was pronounced by Mr. F. to be of good quality for steamboat use. Some pieces which we brought down with us burned very freely, and emitted great heat. Mr. F. thought it a great discovery, and had an inclination to apply to the Chilian government for permission to work the mine. The Buenos Ayrean government, also, I was informed, laid claim to this desolate country. Forest trees, of great size, both of hard and soft wood, appeared to be abundant; and numerous streams of water are convenient, which could readily supply water-power sufficient to manufacture almost any quantity of lumber. A canal might very easily be dug to the straits, or a railroad might be constructed, so as to take the coal, with little trouble, from the mine to the colony. The padre said that an English company, some time ago, started to explore this mine, but, on account of the great depth of snow, gave up the enterprise without inspection.

We returned to the settlement before night, and went to the young officer's house, where we were bountifully supplied with refreshments, and had a very pleasant, sociable interview, into which the priest entered with due spirit, in respect both to the physical and mental refreshments. Returned to the vessel at dusk. The next morning we landed some goods, and traded with the people. The principal articles purchased were cougar-skins, guanaco-skins, and a few ostrich-skins, sewed together in the form of a cape, the long feathers being extracted, leaving a soft, downy surface. The governor asked permission, which the captain readily granted, for some of the women to visit the vessel and trade on board; and in the afternoon half a dozen or more of them visited us, viewed the vessel, purchased such articles as they wanted, and were then set on shore. We spent here a day or two more very agreeably, trading with the convicts and gunning in the vicinity of the settlement. We had a little sport in trying to capture some sea-lions that were gambolling around the vessel, but were unsuccessful. We saw the skin of one that had been captured by one of the convicts; it was black, covered with a thick coat of coarse hair, or rather bristles. In size they were about equal to the common bull-dog. They rise every now and then to the surface of the water, to blow, like a porpoise. We bade the governor, the young officer and the padre, an affectionate farewell. Their kindness and courtesy had made our visit so agreeable that we were almost sorry to leave them. Not long after our departure, we were shocked to learn that they had met with a sudden and cruel fate. The convicts mutinied, and rose upon the officers. The governor and the priest succeeded in reaching the opposite shore, where they remained three days without food. They decided to return to the settlement, and abide the consequences, whatever they might be. The convicts bound them hand and foot, roasted them alive, burned their bones, and danced over their ashes! We had parted from them expecting never again to see their faces, but had loved to think of them as still inhabiting that bleak shore, turning it, by the magic of their cheerful temper, into a pleasant garden, and warming it in the glow of their kindly hearts. Their end was in such fearful contrast to their lives, and did such violence to our remembrance of their virtues, that the tidings affected us with a sense of personal loss, and made that lonely spot at once among the happiest and the saddest of my experience.

CHAPTER XI

Port Famine—St. Nicholas' Bay, and its inscriptions—Politeness of the Indians declined—Difficulty of navigating the straits—A post-bag in a bottle—An English steamer, and its humane errand—Exertions of the British government to rescue prisoners in Patagonia—American schooner—Celebration of our safe passage through the straits—Juan Fernandez—News from home—A chapter of accidents—A trip to Lima—Almost an adventure—Arrival at San Francisco—Journey to the mines—A happy meeting.

Our next stopping-place was Port Famine. We were visited, the first evening after we anchored, by the acting governor of the colony and their Irish doctor. The captain and myself went on shore the next day, and made a very agreeable visit to the officers, who treated us with much politeness. We spent two or three days here. We next cast anchor in Saint Nicholas' Bay, a beautiful harbor. Going on shore, we observed the names of a number of vessels that had preceded us through the straits carved upon trees, with the dates of the several inscriptions; we added our own to the catalogue. There were some deserted bush-huts, probably of Terra-del-Fuegans, who frequently cross over the straits in their canoes, when fishing. A small, shallow stream, of much beauty, flows into the harbor; we rowed up it for some distance, gunning on the banks. From this point, several ineffectual attempts were made to advance; but we were driven back as soon as we cleared Cape Froward, and obliged to retreat to our anchorage. Our vessel was flat, and could not hold on before a stiff breeze, but was inclined, like a crab, to move sideways. The wind having subsided, we made sail late in the afternoon, succeeded in doubling Cape Froward, and dropped anchor in Snug Bay; but, not being pleased with our position, weighed anchor, and continued our course to Fortescue Bay. In passing Cape Holland we saw a large company of Indians. They paraded on the shore with dingy flags flying, and waved skins in the air to invite our approach; but we kept on our way without noticing them; anchored, the next afternoon, in Port Gallant,—a fine harbor, sheltered from all winds. We observed the wreck of some large vessel, and conjectured that it might be that of a French bark of which we were told at Port Famine, which was run ashore and plundered by the Indians, who murdered the crew. We were advised to keep a sharp look-out for Indians here, which we failed not to do; but none made their appearance. As we beat up Crooked Beach, and passed the end of Carlos III. Islands, we discovered a white flag flying on the Terra-del-Fuegan shore. Thinking it might be the signal of some white people who had been shipwrecked, we stood over into the opposite channel, near enough to see Indians and their canoes on the beach, ready to pay us a visit. We hove about, having no desire to make their acquaintance, and anchored, towards night, in the beautiful Borga Bay, opposite.

The most difficult and dangerous feature of navigation in the straits is the encountering of sudden and violent squalls, which strike the vessel without the least warning, and are frequently enough to wreck her in a few minutes even in the hands of the most experienced seamen. We found on shore inscriptions of California-bound vessels, as before. On a branch of a tree overhanging a little stream, we found a bottle suspended, containing papers. This was taken on board, and its contents examined. Three or four vessels, passing through the straits, had left memoranda of their experience,—such as snow-storms, loss of spars, anchors, chains, &c. Captain Morton wrote a humorous account of our voyage, to deposit in this repository of curiosities; and I added a contribution, narrating my capture by the Indians and escape, with a request that, if it should fall into hands bound for the United States or England, it might be published. I little thought that it would bear to my anxious friends the first intelligence of my safety. I left letters at Sea-Lion Island, to be forwarded by the first opportunity, which failed to reach their destination; but this, bottled and suspended from a tree in the wilderness, first fell into the hands of an Indian, who sold it to some passing trader, by whom the soiled writing was deciphered, and kindly forwarded to Smith's News-room, in Boston, and was published in the "Boston Atlas."

Our progress was slow, both wind and tide being against us; a strong current set constantly to the eastward. At Swallow Harbor, where we next anchored, we were completely sheltered from the winds, except that which came down from the lofty mountains, called by the sailors "willewaws." The scenery around is exceedingly wild. There was a beautiful waterfall on the mountain side, the stream probably fed by melting snow. We stopped at many harbors as we passed along, most of them quite secure when entered, but difficult of access. Half-port Bay, at which we touched, is very properly named. It is but a slight indentation in the land, and has a bottom affording very poor holding-ground, covered with kelp; besides, it is very imperfectly sheltered from the wind. While lying here we had a severe gale from the westward, which produced considerable "chop." Our vessel dragged her anchors, in consequence of their becoming foul with kelp. However, by dropping our kedge-anchor, and loading the chains, we succeeded in arresting our motion before striking the rocks. We had a narrow escape.

At Cape Monday, having cast anchor, we discovered, towards night, a steamer on the Patagonian side, bound westward. Our colors were set, as there were indications of a dark and stormy night, and the steamer turned about and steered for our harbor. This was a pleasant circumstance, as the captain meant, if possible, to get towed through the straits. The vessel anchored near us, and proved to be the Fire Fly, Captain Smith master, built for an English gentleman residing in Talchuana, and now bound to Valparaiso. Captain Smith had his daughter with him, and half a dozen passengers. We visited them, and were very civilly received, invited into the cabin, and introduced to the young lady. On hearing my name, she observed that they found at Borga Bay a paper in a bottle, describing the captivity of a person bearing the same name in Patagonia, with an account of his escape. Captain Morton informed her that I was the writer of that document. "Is it possible?" she exclaimed; "then you are the hero of those adventures!" "I certainly am the unfortunate person there described," I replied, "though wholly undeserving the name of hero." She expressed, as did all the passengers, much sympathy, and asked many questions in regard to the treatment received and the life led during my captivity.

Captain Smith suggested that I might be able to give him some information in regard to two Englishmen who had been captured by the savages. He had orders from the Board of Admiralty to make search at any places at which he might touch on the Patagonian coast, and endeavor to learn something of their fate. I told him that I knew something of certain English prisoners in that country, and proceeded to relate what I had learned from the Indians of the murder of Captain Eaton, and the capture and subsequent murder of Messrs. Sims and Douglass; giving the names of the vessel and the prisoners from information communicated by Mr. Hall. Captain Smith produced his letter of instructions, and the names and circumstances perfectly coincided, except that the instructions described the Avon as a ship, while she was styled by Mr. Hall as a brig; an immaterial variation, as all classes of vessels often pass under the general designation of "ships." My deposition of the facts was written out by two of the passengers, and, having been read to me, I signed it, for transmission to England. The English government, Captain Smith said, had been at great pains and expense to obtain information of those unfortunate young men, who belonged to highly respectable families in England, and to facilitate their escape. Boats had been sent out and buried in the sand, and a great number of handkerchiefs had been printed, containing particular statements of the situation of the buried boats; these had been distributed to vessels bound near the Patagonian coast, to be thrown ashore, in the hope that they might be picked up by Indians, and thus convey the desired information to the prisoners, if they were living. In hearing what the British government had done for its unfortunate subjects, I indulged in some bitter remarks on the supposed neglect of our government in respect to my fate, in leaving me (as I presumed to think) to perish among cannibals, without making any effort to learn my fate, or to rescue me from destruction; remarks of which I had abundant cause to be ashamed, when I learned what had been actually attempted in my behalf.

We could effect no arrangement to be towed by the steamer, as the captain said his stock of fuel was too small to warrant running the risk of being retarded; besides, in case of accident, it would affect his insurance. We spent part of the evening on board the steamer; very soon after returning to our ship, a boat, containing two or three of the passengers, drew up alongside, and a package was put into my hands containing ten dollars, and a letter, signed by the captain and passengers, requesting my acceptance of the gift, as a slight token of their regard and sympathy. While returning my hearty thanks for such a demonstration of kindness to a stranger, I begged to decline the money; but they urged its acceptance, and I reluctantly gratified their wishes.

All the next day we beat along, till we found anchorage at Round Island for the night. On nearing the harbor, a mast was observed on the rocks, lying partly out of the water. I took the boat, early the next morning, to ascertain if it was attached to a wreck; but found that it was loose, and must have drifted there. I knocked off the iron band and cross-trees from the mast-head, and brought them on board our vessel. At Tamer Harbor, our next port, we noticed the wreck of a new vessel, lying well up on the shore, her bottom badly shattered by the rocks on which she had been driven, and both masts gone; it proved to be the "John A. Sutter," of Rhode Island. On the opposite shore were parts of iron-mills, and other machinery, probably designed for use in California. The shore was strewed with trunks and chests, from the wreck; she had been stripped of everything valuable. The cabin on deck had been cut, and partially burned, by those touching at the harbor. We fished up a bundle of steel rods from the hold, which was partly filled with sand and water. The vessel had been wrecked, as we afterwards ascertained, in a thick fog, on one of the little islands off the western mouth of the straits, and drifted back to the harbor, where we found her. While we were here, the schooner Julius Pringle, of New London, bound to California, came in and anchored. The next day a fine wind bore us to Mercy Harbor, the last anchorage in the Straits of Magellan. The harbor is a good one; and we determined not to leave it till we had a good wind, that would take us well out, far enough to clear the islands lying off the north side. We remained several days waiting for a south-westerly wind, during which delay a pilot-boat, bound for the golden country, came up with us. Our time here was spent very agreeably; our passage through the straits had consumed fifty-one days, and had been effected without accident, though we had witnessed repeated tokens of disaster to some of our predecessors. By way of celebrating our success, we got up a "clam-bake," minus the clams, in lieu of which we collected and roasted a quantity of muscles, by burying them in the earth, and applying hot stones; they proved excellent eating, and we had "a good time."

Our mate, who was a sensible young man, of good education, had two foibles; he was a decided grumbler, and, in his conviviality, he was a little too far from total abstinence. He had a particular dislike of a dog on board, purchased at Sandy Point,—a thievish rascal, that always had his nose in anything that was dirty; even the tar and slush-buckets did not escape his attentions. On the evening of the clam-bake, the mate was a little exhilarated; and, having pulled off his pea-jacket preparatory to "turning in" for the night, he seized Bose, mistaking him for the jacket he had just dropped, and threw him into his berth. The dog was not at all displeased with such comfortable quarters, and lay down very nicely with his unexpected bed-fellow. I observed the mate, the next morning, sitting near his berth, yawning; his eyes presently rested on the detested Bose; his feet were in quick motion, and an unceremonious kick turned the dog out as suddenly as he had been turned in. The incident afforded us a hearty laugh at the mate's expense, who became, for the rest of the voyage, a decided temperance man.

Tired of our detention, we put off in unfavorable weather; the Pringle and the pilot-boat (whose name I have forgotten) getting out with us, but we found it expedient to retreat to our anchorage. A gale soon followed, which prolonged our stay; when its fury was past, we got out and proceeded northward, for Callao. In passing the port of Juan Fernandez, we saw a whaling-ship just putting out to sea; we had designed to stop here for some supplies, but concluded that we could better obtain them at Callao, and held on our course. In our way to Callao we spoke the bark Sarah, Captain Morse, from New Bedford, bound to California with a company of sixty members, of which Captain Morse was president. Our captain told them that he had on board a man from New Bedford,—Captain Bourne,—escaped from captivity among the Indians. Captain Morse replied that he recollected the sloop of war Vandalia was sent down to the straits in search of him. Presently a crowd of persons surrounded the captain of the Sarah, who appeared to be talking earnestly; the bark was soon hove to, and several gentlemen from New Bedford came to us in a boat. They seemed overjoyed to find me alive and well, and made numerous inquiries about my captivity and rescue. They informed me that the Vandalia was despatched by our government to my relief, with orders to punish my captors, if expedient and practicable. From them, also, I gained the first information concerning my ship and shipmates; it seemed that the vessel, with the Hebe and the J. B. Gager, lost their chains and anchors in the straits, and dragged out to sea. The John Allyne, after steering two or three days for Montevideo, to repair and obtain supplies, ascertained that they had water enough aboard to carry them around Cape Horn, the only practicable course, as, without chains and anchors, it was impossible to enter the straits. With the concurrence of all on board, it was decided to attempt the passage round the cape as they were. They encountered a gale off the Horn; and, while lying to, the vessel was knocked on her beam ends. The second mate, Mr. F. Crapo, of New Bedford, was washed overboard, and lost; others were badly bruised, some narrowly escaping the doom of the mate. The cabin partly filled with water; but the schooner righted, with the loss of spars, sails, bulwarks, caboose, and stanchions. She finally weathered the gale, and arrived at Valparaiso, forty-one days after I was left in Patagonia. Here the vessel was repaired, at great cost, and proceeded safely to California. After the relation of this chapter of accidents, I gave them a brief narrative of my adventures among the Patagonians; they returned towards night to their ship. The wind was light, and in the morning we were still near each other; several of the passengers came to us in a boat, bringing with them a quantity of American newspapers. I found in them notices of the disasters that befell my vessel, and the particulars of my capture. The papers were lent to me until we should meet at Callao,—a great favor; their contents were devoured with a high relish, as they were the first American papers I had seen since my capture. Both vessels arrived safely, on the third day afterwards, at Callao.

In the evening after our arrival, I went with the captain and Mr. F. on board the Sarah, and spent an hour very agreeably. The passengers had agreed to take the diligence next morning, and visit the city of Lima, six miles distant, and they invited us to join them. Mr. F. assented, but I declined, preferring, on the whole, to remain on shipboard. The party were on shore betimes the next morning, except Mr. F., who consumed so much time in urging me to go with them, in which Captain Morton joined, that he said the company must have got off; and, unless I would accompany him on horseback, he would have to bear me company in the ship; so, rather than disappoint him, though caring but little personally for the jaunt, I yielded. We went ashore immediately, procured horses, and, having found our friends, rambled over the city, viewing the numerous public buildings by which it is adorned. We were continually beset by shrivelled, cadaverous beggars; they posted themselves at every corner, and besought us, by the Blessed Virgin, to give them alms. The day passed, on the whole, so pleasantly, and there remained so many objects of interest unvisited, we rather regretted that it was not longer. The diligence drove up to the hotel towards evening, to take our friends to the port; we started for our horses, intending to overtake and accompany them in their drive, but missed our way. Some time elapsed before we found ourselves at the gate of the city, opening on the beautiful public road to Callao. As we passed out, we drew up at a respectable-looking ranche; two young Spaniards appeared to be the only occupants. With some little delay, during which one of the two stepped out at a back door, we procured cigars, lighted them, and were moving towards the entrance. Whilst I was paying for them, my companion got the start of me. As I was placing my foot in the stirrup, twenty or thirty mounted horsemen dashed through the gateway, up to the house. They were armed to the teeth; their holsters stuck full of pistols, and I could see shining blades protruding through their garments. They had a desperate, lawless look, unlike that of soldiers or civil officers, and it seemed to me they were no better than they should be. I thought of the delay in giving us our cigars, and it struck me that one of the troop strongly resembled the fellow who stepped out so quietly on our entrance. I sprang into the saddle and gave my horse two or three smart raps, under the stimulus of which he cleared the causeway between the sidewalk and the road at a single bound, and speedily overtook my companion. He had caught a glimpse of the armed cavalcade, and we urged our horses at full speed for about a mile, without looking back. On turning, nothing was seen but a long streak of dust. We then compared notes touching the armed men, and agreed that we were best off at a distance from them. We made the best of our way to Callao, which we reached a little after dark, and found the captain delighted at our safe return, as he had feared some accident, having heard since morning of several robberies lately committed on that road. He had been told that a perfect understanding existed between the robbers and the people of Callao, who gave daily intelligence of persons leaving the port for the city; and that even officers of the government were suspected of conniving at these outrages, if not actually in league with the banditti. As yet, all attempts to ferret them out and break up their combination had failed. Our description of the party we encountered so far agreed with the statements of American residents at Callao, that we were congratulated, and felt disposed to congratulate ourselves, on our safe journey. Neither of us was burdened with plata, and we had no more effective weapons than our jack-knives.

As a national vessel had been ordered to the coast of Patagonia for my relief, I thought it my duty to report myself the next day to the American consul, who was much interested by the recital of my experience. The brig Ann and Julia, Captain McAlister, of New Orleans, came into port a day or two after. Captain McAlister said that the Vandalia came into Rio Janeiro while he was there, shipped more men, and sailed southward in great haste.

Having obtained wood and water and other necessary supplies, we put out to sea once more. I must not omit to record the kindness shown, and the still greater kindness tendered me, by the captain of the

Sarah, and all the members of the company. They offered me a free passage and any assistance I might need on arrival in California; but the generosity of Captain Morton had supplied all present needs, and, with all gratitude for their proffered aid, I was not willing to tax their bounty in advance. We stood well to the westward before crossing the line, as only light winds can be expected before reaching from five to seven degrees of north or south latitude, when the trade-winds set in. We had a passage of thirty-seven days from Callao to San Francisco, which was in very good time, considering the sailing qualities of our vessel. We anchored in the beautiful harbor, February 19, 1850, one year and seven days from the date of my leaving New Bedford.

Any description of San Francisco would be altogether superfluous, as her streets, even, are familiar in the states as household words. I found, upon going ashore, letters from those most dear to me, which had long awaited my arrival; also one from a brother then in California. He stated that immediately on hearing of my misfortunes he started for San Francisco to see Commodore Jones, then on that station, and endeavor to induce him to make an effort for my release. On making his business known, the gallant commodore informed him that he had already heard of it, and had despatched the sloop-of-war Levant for my rescue, in the full confidence that the enterprise would be successful. When I was telling the Indian council that flourishing story of my consequence at home, and of the big ships and little ships, the big guns and little guns, that were at my command, ready to avenge any mischief they might do me, I little thought how literally the action of our government, and the spontaneous kindness of Commodore Jones, were verifying my words. The sympathy manifested in my behalf by the gallant commodore deserves more than this passing notice. My brother also left a deposit of funds against my arrival, if it ever occurred, of the probability of which he was in some doubt; also his address, and that of another brother, who was then at the mines. I could learn but little as to the fate of my vessel, or of my effects on board, except that she had duly arrived there, and, after much disagreement and dispute among the company, had been sold for a trifle above the costs of repair on the passage. This operation, I thought, savored little of Yankee shrewdness; since we arrived at a later date, with a vessel of about the same size, age and value, at a time when shipping was in less demand, and sold her for nearly three times the amount. I was happy to meet many acquaintances, who gave me a hearty welcome, and showed me kindness I can never forget.

The schooner J. Pringle, from which we parted on issuing from the Straits of Magellan, arrived in port very soon after us, having touched at Valparaiso. Her captain said that he found the sloop-of-war Vandalia at Valparaiso, to obtain chains and an anchor, as she had lost one anchor and one hundred and thirty fathoms of chain in Possession Bay, and was obliged to double Cape Horn. She was to sail again for Patagonia as soon as the damages were repaired, entering the western mouth of the straits. Captain B. reported my escape, and that I was safe on board the Hopewell, for California, informing the officers that he parted company with me at Mercy Harbor—intelligence that was received with demonstrations of lively pleasure.

Being unable to obtain any information of my personal effects, left on the John Allyne, I left this mushroom city on the third day after my arrival, and took passage in the steamer Senator for Sacramento, at the moderate fare of twenty-five dollars for a passage of a few hours' duration. I found this city of rag houses full of the indications of its recent and rapid settlement. The streets abounded in mud, a foot or more in depth. Here I recovered my chest, but the trunks containing my clothing were missing. Our company, it appeared, had broken up, and its members were dispersed hither and thither in the mines, every man for himself. My brothers, as near as I could ascertain, were seventy miles distant, possibly removed to the Middle Fork of the American river, and I decided to start on foot. Accordingly, having purchased, at enormous prices, a pair of red flannel blankets, thick boots, a rifle and revolver, and other necessary equipments, I set out for the mines the next morning, in company with two or three persons from the States. The road was exceedingly muddy, but materially improved after passing Sutter's Fort. We had travelled ten miles, when I found that my feet were so badly blistered that I could proceed no further, and advised my companions to go on without me. My feet were in fact almost completely skinned. After resting at a public-house till the next morning, and encasing my sore feet in a pair of poor, thin shoes, I pursued my journey. I made very slow progress. An ox-team overtook me, the owner of which kept a house, or, more properly speaking, a booth, for boarding and lodging miners, five or six miles ahead. He kindly offered me a ride, which I gladly accepted, and lodged with him for the night.

My journey the next day was less fatiguing; on the day following I arrived at Georgetown, where I found that my brothers had built them a house and spent the winter, but had now left the place, and removed to the Middle Fork. The distance was twenty miles by one route and fifteen by another. The longest road was considered the best, and I followed it, lodging at night in a low grog-shop, denominated an inn. A snow-storm detained me here during the next forenoon. By noon it appeared to have cleared up, and I resumed my march, but had not gone more than a mile before it began snowing again, as fast as before; yet I was resolved not to turn back. The snow, however, fell so fast, and with increasing violence, and the road was so wretched, that this resolution was somewhat shaken. The way led through a forest of lofty pines, the land broken by deep gulches and high hills. As I trudged along through the deep snow, my attention was suddenly attracted to a clump of bushes by the wayside, that appeared to wave to and fro, as if agitated by something more than wind. I felt for my knife and pistol, to make sure they were where they could be made immediately available, placed my hand on the lock of my rifle, and awaited in silence the approach of my unseen visitor. Presently a pair of large, glistening eyes glared at me through an opening in the bushes. Nothing else was discernible; the form, and even the head, of the animal to whom these fierce optics appertained, could not be made out. But their gaze was fixed steadily upon me, and I returned it with equal steadiness, if not equal brilliancy and effect, without once changing my position. I had heard of looking wild animals out of countenance, and determined to try the experiment, before resorting to any other decisive measures. After gazing fixedly at the mysterious occupant of the thicket for a few minutes, he turned and walked leisurely away, giving me only an imperfect view of his figure. So far as I could distinguish the shape, it appeared to be a grisly bear, though not of the largest size. I was glad to get rid of so ugly a customer on such easy terms, and went on my way rejoicing, though it was a weary and desolate one.

Being very much fatigued, I halted at the foot of a large oak-tree, as the shades of evening were closing around me, with the design of climbing it, and spending the night as comfortably as I could in its branches,—the lodging that I had anticipated might be the only available one. But, after a few minutes' rest, I roused my flagging energies and concluded to feel—for I could not see—my way a little further, before roosting for the night. The darkness of the night, deepened by the storm, hid the path so effectually, that the Yankee faculty of guessing was called into abundant exercise. I trudged along, however, with dogged determination, which was very soon rewarded. Half a mile had scarcely been passed, when a bright light greeted me, issuing from a tent. Walking up to it, I found it occupied by three men, emigrants from the vicinity of my native place. They cordially welcomed and hospitably entertained me, on learning who I was, and promised me every assistance in their power.

The next morning I set out again, and reached the river. I was at no loss to designate the spot where my brothers were likely to be found, but a formidable barrier interposed: a rapid and swollen stream separated us, just as we were almost within speaking distance. I walked along the shore to find a log or some wood with which to construct a float; nothing could be found. It was a grievous disappointment;

my evil star, I thought, had not yet waned. At the opposite shore, fastened to the branch of a tree, lay a snug little raft, as if in mockery. I must spend the night, it seemed, on the river banks, without food or shelter, and within sight of my friends. Just before night I was fortunate enough to descry a man on the further shore, who appeared to be on the look-out for some one, and hailed him. He answered, and forthwith took me over. I was soon in the presence of my two brothers, neither of whom at first recognized me. It was a happy meeting, and on their part wholly unexpected, as they had given me up for lost. After many congratulations and innumerable questions, rapidly interchanged, I mentioned the difficulty I had in making the last stage of the journey to them,—the passage of the river. They said that they were on the look-out that evening for one of their number: otherwise, I might have staid there a week without attracting the attention of anybody. They congratulated me on my ill success in searching for a log, or the materials to construct a float. The attempt to cross would have been extremely hazardous, and very likely fatal. The river was full of rapids, eccentric currents, and other perils, making it at all times difficult to cross, with the best facilities that could be commanded. Of all this I had ample confirmation in no long time after. Two men started to paddle themselves over in a canoe at the same place. Before they reached the opposite shore, their canoe was borne down the stream into the rapids, and dashed to pieces against the rocks. One of them was drowned; the other caught the top of a small tree just before reaching the rapids. By collecting all the ropes and lines we could find, attaching a stone to one end and throwing it within his reach, the means of rescue, after several trials, were put into his power. Such was the roar of the waters we could not speak in tones audible by him, but made signs to him to secure the rope about his body, and he was drawn to the shore in safety. A similar accident afterwards happened to one of my brothers, in attempting to cross with another man upon a raft. The swift current drifted them within the power of the rapids, and it was only by the greatest exertions that they escaped the boiling abyss below.

CHAPTER XII

A gigantic speculation, with a dwarfish result—Perils of waters—Sickness and bereavement—Growth of Sacramento and San Francisco—Voyage homeward—Imposition on shipboard—Panama—Havana—Home—Concluding observations—Practicability of Christian missions in Patagonia considered.

On my arrival at the mines, I found my brothers engaged in a company of twenty men, organized for the purpose of tunnelling a mountain ridge, and digging a raceway at its base, with a view to dam the river and turn it through the tunnel. By this means the bed of the river, for a mile or more, would be laid bare, and gold in great profusion, it was believed, would be discovered. Nineteen of the members were on the ground; the twentieth was unable to come; and, though there were several applicants for the vacancy, I was chosen to fill it. We commenced operations in about a week. It may give a clearer idea of the magnitude of the work, to state that an excavation, twelve feet wide by seven deep, was made, by blasting through rock (slate and granite) a distance of over a hundred feet. The race was nearly half a mile in length; the prices paid for every article of food were enormous. Before turning the river, we let out the expected field of gold to be worked by seven hundred men, who were to give us one-half of the produce; there was great expectation. The work was the greatest of this nature that had yet been undertaken in California; we had worked hard through a whole season, and brought it to a successful completion, without any fatal accident, though several dangerous circumstances had threatened to retard its progress. Everything being prepared, the dam was closed, the river rose,—pressed, as if angrily, against the new barrier that opposed its wonted flow,—and then sullenly explored the novel course that solicited its waters. The dry channel was eagerly attacked; but, alas for human hopes! it proved to be anything but rich; in fact, it was less favorable for working than the average, and the diggers abandoned the spot, leaving the company chagrined, and greatly disheartened at their fruitless conclusion.

I came very near being delivered from this disappointment, and from all other earthly cares,—those of authorship included,—by a hasty trip into the rapids. During the intervals of our work, a young man of the company undertook with me to construct a canoe, and establish a ferry for passengers across the river. Our skiff, on its completion, was carried by all hands to the river bank, and committed to the stream, with all the ceremonies customary on the launching of larger craft. A successful adventure was made, the next day, with one passenger. On the following day six miners applied for passage; I took half of them on board, with their picks, pans and shovels, and started with them. We had approached within ten feet of the opposite bank, when a counter-current suddenly struck us, whirled the head of the boat from the direction of the shore, and, in spite of the utmost exertion, carried us into the stream, and almost over the rapids. By a successful manoeuvre we turned her head up stream, and paddled moderately till we had passed the dangerous spot. At length, after a great struggle with imminent danger, in the midst of which the passengers were praying and crying for mercy and help, we reached some trees, standing in the swollen stream. By taking hold of one of the branches the boat was brought to, but with such violence as to dash in her side; we sprang safely into the trees as soon as the boat struck. Our friends on shore cut poles, and extended them to us, by help of which we were soon on terra firma. Our boat rolled over, and sunk. An attack of dysentery soon after interrupted my work, but not for a great length of time.

After the failure of our river speculation, I spent some time "prospecting" for a desirable "digging." Before one was discovered that offered much inducement, I was again prostrated by illness, during which my brothers joined me, with the mournful intelligence that my little son was no more! These heavy tidings, at such a time, proved almost too much for an enfeebled body and anxious mind; it was the thought of my little family that nerved my spirit against despair, in the darkest hours of captivity. A blow there turned my strength into weakness, and my weakness well-nigh into absolute helplessness.

It would be too far from the purpose of this volume to solicit the reader's company through all my wanderings for a year and a half in this wonderful country, to which so many high hopes are carried, and from which so many sad disappointments are daily borne. It is enough to say that I had six successive attacks of sickness, the last the most severe of all; I was brought to death's door, and had little hope of seeing home again. After a month's illness, my medical attendant advised a return to the States, as soon as I could bear the exercise of riding. At the earliest day prudence would allow, I was carried, with all practicable care, to Sacramento, a city I had not seen since I passed through it a year and a half before. Its appearance was greatly improved in every respect. With the increased supply of necessaries and conveniences, the fabulous prices of eighteen months before had given place to more sober, authentic, and matter-of-fact demands; steamboat fare had fallen from twenty-five dollars to one, and the crowding and shouting of runners compared with the most active scenes of the kind to be witnessed in New York or Albany. We arrived at San Francisco during the night; as the day dawned, and the mist that covered the town was lifted, the spectacle that met the view was like enchantment; a compact and well-built city had risen, its beautiful harbor lined with extensive wharves, spacious warehouses, and elegant dwellings, fronting upon broad streets, and all appliances of business and pleasure offering themselves in profusion.

I walked to the nearest hotel, as I was too feeble to go a hundred yards. The friend who accompanied me, and took upon himself all care of the voyage in respect to both of us, found that the steamers were crowded to the utmost, and engaged passage in a bark for San Juan del Sud, or Panama. We examined the printed bill of fare, and thought it would be very satisfactory, if its promises were fulfilled. I noticed, however, that the potatoes on board were of bad quality, and suggested the propriety of raising a committee of passengers to investigate the stores; but the motion was overruled as unnecessary.

We put to sea with about a hundred and thirty passengers, many of whom suffered severely from sea-sickness. These improved in a few days, and began to feel like eating; but, to their consternation, instead of wholesome provisions and fresh water, nothing was to be had but spoiled meat, and water that was unfit to drink, having been put up in old beer-casks and become tainted,—and a short allowance of that. We were stinted to three pints a day each for drinking and culinary purposes. The only wholesome and eatable articles of food were pork, bread and dried apples. Tea and coffee were too wretched to be used. Those wiseacres who had so summarily declined any examination of the provisions before starting now came to me with very long faces, confessing their error when it was too late to be remedied. For forty-eight days they languished on this miserable fare. There were many quarrels and contentions on board, growing out of these difficulties, and some cases of sickness. We buried two men at sea and one the day after our arrival in port; and the whole company, in fact, were little better than skeletons when they reached San Juan. As to myself, my appetite craved but little food, and the sea air agreed so well with me that I had almost recovered on arrival there.

We mounted mules on the following day, and crossed to Lake Nicaragua, which we reached just too late for the steamer. Some of the company went up the lake and procured small sail to take them across, but I decided to remain till the arrival of another regular steamer from San Francisco. This detained us two weeks, when we proceeded to Georgetown, on the Atlantic shore, and took passage on board the steamer Daniel Webster, for New York, via Havana. As we passed out of the harbor a salute was fired for the United States steamer Saranac, then visiting that port to investigate the affair of the British brig Express firing into one of our steamers a short time before, on account of a refusal to pay certain port charges. When fairly outside the bar, the tables were set, and the hungry passengers had begun fortifying their stomachs with eager emulation, when I perceived a commotion among the officers and men betokening something wrong. Presently the head pump was working lively, and the men appeared, running with buckets of water. To the questions rained upon them they made no reply, but hastened along in silence. The boat had taken fire, but it was promptly extinguished before many of the passengers suspected it.

On arrival at Havana we anchored, after dark, under the walls of the fort, and our fires were allowed to go out. During the night a breeze sprung up, producing a swell in the harbor, which rendered our position a dangerous one, as there was not room for the boat to swing around clear of the rocks. The passengers all felt extremely anxious for their safety; but the fires were renewed, sufficient steam was soon generated to work the ponderous engine, the steamer swung slowly and safely around, and we were safe. The Spanish guard-boats ordered us back to our first anchorage, but the captain replied that he was master of the vessel and should put her in a place of safety.

The next morning we took in coal and started for New York. I was seized, on the following day, for the first time in my life, with chills and fever, but partially recovered, under care of the ship's physician, before arriving in port. We made New York without accident, and having spent two days in the city, the steamer State of Maine bore me to my home, January 13th, 1852,—after an absence of three years, lacking a month,—with a heart rising gratefully to God for his many interpositions in my behalf, to deliver me from the perils of the sea and the perils of the land.

It can scarcely be necessary, for the benefit of any reader who has followed me through the course of this narrative, to add any remarks on the hazards of visiting Patagonia, or the consequences likely to ensue in the event of shipwreck on that desolate coast. The land is dreary, and it were a sufficient trial of fortitude to be cast away upon it,—to run the imminent risk of perishing by cold, and hunger and thirst. But the extremest peril arising from the poverty of the country is exhilarating, compared with the tender mercies of the people. Rather than trust to their protection, better hide from the light of day and gnaw the bark of stunted trees for food, drinking, as I did, from the briny sea. The dread which has deterred voyagers from entering the country, or even touching the shore, unless armed to the teeth, offering articles of traffic with one hand and holding a loaded musket in the other, is no more than reasonable. I do not know that the country has ever been explored by civilized man. The officers and men of the Adventure and Beagle, two ships sent out by the British Admiralty to survey the Straits of Magellan in the years 1826, 1830, 1832 and 1834, examined and penetrated the country to a greater extent than any other voyagers.

If the other tribes inhabiting the country resemble that with which I was domesticated, it must be a hazardous enterprise for missionaries to attempt the propagation of the gospel among them. Even apart from this, the difficulty of gaining a subsistence there must prove an almost insuperable obstacle. The barrenness of the soil, and the want of water, render agriculture a desperate resource, and there is no spontaneous product of the earth to sustain life. To live like the savages would be simply impossible to men who have been habituated to the comforts of civilized life; I could not have survived many months of such hardship. Provisions would have to be imported; this difficulty seems sufficient to discourage, if not to prevent, efforts in that direction. When, to this, we add the cruelty, the duplicity, the treachery and blood-thirstiness of the people, I am unable to conjecture through what direct agency they can be reached by the influences of Christianity. Whether access to them could be gained through their Spanish American neighbors, or by enticing some of them, when young, into a more civilized society, and so opening an avenue of peaceable and beneficial intercourse, it is not easy to conclude, without actual experiment.

Since returning to this country, these views have been confirmed, by the narrative recently published of the sad fate of the English missionaries sent to Patagonia. Captain Gardiner, and three or four Cornish fishermen, who volunteered for this labor of love, were landed by a passing vessel somewhere, on the inhospitable coast. So inveterate was the hostility of the natives, they durst not trust themselves among them; they were driven, in their covered barges, from place to place; like their Master, having not, on the land, where to lay their heads. Arrangements had been made, before leaving England, to have provisions follow them; thirty-six barrels of provisions, destined for them, were found some time after, by a government vessel, at the Falkland Islands. The commander took them on board, and sailed for the place of their destination; upon their first landing, traces of the unfortunate men were found; and, on thorough search, directions were discovered to look for them at another place. They were followed from one stopping-place to another, till the grave of one of them was found, who had died of starvation. The survivors were traced to a spot where their boats lay on the shore, unoccupied; at a little distance off lay their bodies, unburied, their bones bleaching on the sand. The humane discoverers buried their remains. On lifting a stone from the mouth of a cave, there was disclosed a narrative of their sufferings, and of successive deaths, written by Captain Gardiner; at the date of the last entry he had not tasted food for four days. In all probability, he shared the fate of his brethren,—starvation,—and with him closed their melancholy history. A sad tale! Yet there were days and weeks when I would have gladly exchanged my lot for wanderings like theirs, upon the desert shore. But from those horrors I was mercifully delivered; they, in the prosecution of a sacred and benevolent errand, were cut down by the dispensation of Him who seeth not as man seeth.

It may occur to some reader that the deceptions I practised upon the natives, as frankly narrated, had a tendency to impair their confidence in white men, and thus to increase the difficulty of reaching them by Christian influences, and to render the lot of any poor man hereafter falling into their hands more desperate than it would otherwise be. Perhaps so; yet the danger does not seem so imminent, when we consider that they are entire strangers to truth. Probably no Patagonian's experience or observation could furnish an example of consistent veracity, and they would not be likely to suspect the existence of such a virtue in any one. It is apparent, from their behavior in the "last scene of all" with me, that from first to last they vehemently mistrusted my statements; and their most likely comment on the report of the chief must have been, "I told you so." The shock was less than if they had reposed a more generous confidence.

The notoriety which was given to my capture by the newspaper press called forth many expressions of sympathy from persons who knew nothing of me, except that I was a fellow-being in distress. To all such I tender my thanks. It is a grateful duty, in parting company with the reader, to renew the expression of thankful remembrance with which I recall the benefactors who, under God, rescued and befriended me,—Mr. Hall, and the noble-hearted captains, who fed and clothed me when hungry and naked, and conveyed me gratuitously to my destination. Nor can I forget the prompt action of the Honorable Secretary of the Navy, the efficient exertions of the officers of the Vandalia, or the generosity of Commodore Jones. I would also acknowledge, with the liveliest gratitude, my obligations to the Hon. Daniel Webster,* the Hon. R. C. Winthrop, the Hon. George Evans, of Maine, and to the Hon. Joseph Grinnell, and the Hon. John H. Clifford, of New Bedford;—all of whom, when informed of my captivity, volunteered their aid, and made those representations to the Navy department which resulted in the despatch of the Vandalia on her humane mission. Nor must I omit to add my thanks to Mr. Denison, who kindly bore their memorials to Washington, and laid them before the department. If I acquired nothing more by my unlooked-for experience, I at least gained a warmer patriotism, and a profounder sense of the benignant wisdom of Providence.

*Since this was written he has passed beyond the reach of my thanks; but this fact cannot suppress the utterance of gratitude which I owe to his august memory.

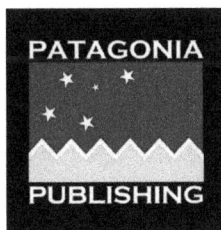

PATAGONIA

PUBLISHING

www.ingramcontent.com/pod-product-compliance
Lightning Source LLC
Chambersburg PA
CBHW060141050426
42448CB00010B/2234